Exceptional People

Lessons Learned from Special Education Survivors

Faith E. Andreasen

ROWMAN & LITTLEFIELD EDUCATION
A division of
ROWMAN & LITTLEFIELD PUBLISHERS, INC.
Lanham • New York • Toronto • Plymouth, UK

Published by Rowman & Littlefield Education
A division of Rowman & Littlefield Publishers, Inc.
A wholly owned subsidiary of The Rowman & Littlefield Publishing Group, Inc.
4501 Forbes Boulevard, Suite 200, Lanham, Maryland 20706
www.rowman.com

10 Thornbury Road, Plymouth PL6 7PP, United Kingdom

British Library Cataloguing in Publication Information Available

Library of Congress Cataloging-in-Publication Data

Andreasen, Faith E., 1956–
Exceptional people : lessons learned from special education survivors / Faith E. Andreasen.
  p. cm.
Includes bibliographical references.
ISBN 978-1-4758-0125-5 (cloth : alk. paper) -- ISBN 978-1-4758-0126-2 (pbk. : alk. paper) -- ISBN 978-1-4758-0127-9 (electronic)
1. Special education--United States--Case studies. 2. Learning disabled children--Education--United States--Case studies. 3. Parents of children with disabilities--United States--Case studies. I. Title.
LC3981.A72 2012
371.9--dc23
2012028663

The paper used in this publication meets the minimum requirements of American National Standard for Information Sciences Permanence of Paper for Printed Library Materials, ANSI/NISO Z39.48-1992.

Printed in the United States of America

Contents

Foreword

"Your feelings matter here." Dr. Andreasen first got my attention in 1997 when she stated this simple premise to a highly impacted sixth-grade boy in our New Mexico school. Not only did she say it, but her actions proved that she meant it, and she became one of the few staff members who could effectively reach this student.

It wasn't that she coddled or encouraged excuses in her classroom of students with emotional and/or behavioral disabilities. Quite the opposite. She set high standards for social and academic performance, in the context of clear expectations and guidelines, and remained determinedly positive about the students' abilities, despite their own learned helplessness, self-disparagement, or lack of support from the home environment.

In fact, I sometimes reflected that with her physically small stature, unflagging integrity, and powerhouse energy for the good of her students, Dr. Andreasen reminded me of a classy version of Mammy Yokum from the *Li'l Abner* comics (Al Capp, 1909–1979). She didn't smoke a cigar or pack a punch, but she wasn't intimidated by belligerent or aggressive behavior, accusing or irrational parents or administrators, or a student's daunting criminal record. Her unwavering certainty that the students could achieve was not only contagious, it was backed up by a solid teaching practice and multifaceted approach.

Intrigued and impressed by her courage and commitment, I worked with her as often as possible for several years until we both relocated. Now I am thrilled to have this opportunity to endorse her book. It doesn't surprise me in the least that this remarkable teacher is still advocating for students' voices to be heard and included as parents and teachers navigate the often bewildering and legalistic world of special education. The message is sorely needed today. Consider my own experience consulting with a classroom teacher as she voiced concerns about a student who was standing right in front of her, with the teacher's hand actually resting on top of the student's head. Interestingly, once we took the time to query the student, we learned that her behavior was rooted in a cause-and-effect rationale, such that addressing this sequence helped us (and her) to positively change the behavior.

Dr. Andreasen understood intuitively what cognitive psychologists have asserted and proven through years of research: we all have ideas, beliefs, feelings, needs, and impressions that form a filter or frame through which we process information from the world and respond to it accordingly. She also realized how important it is to get "buy-in" from students by including them in discussions related to their academic day and broader educational outcome. In short, it stands to reason that taking the time to get students' perspectives will increase the likelihood of greater effort on their part and eventual success of interventions provided by adult caregivers.

In *Exceptional People: Lessons Learned from Special Education Survivors*, Dr. Andreasen depicts the views of a diverse array of students, parents, and teachers and conveys the real-life aftermath of years of concentrated effort on the part of professional educators and families. She also addresses the more difficult social topics with which students are preoccupied, but into which adults prefer not to delve. This is a window into special education that is seldom, if ever, explored in real depth. An alternative title might be "Real Life beyond the IEP."

In addition, and perhaps more importantly, she provides clear, succinct recommendations for adults working with exceptional students, based on these interviews as well as her own twenty years of experience, in a list format that is easily accessed and implemented.

We should all be very grateful that Dr. Andreasen has compiled these case studies so that parents and educators can understand how compelling, revealing, and important a student's thoughts truly are, if only we take the time to ask. The "Tips for Teachers and for Parents" shed light on aspects of a student's educational plan in the greater context of the student's unique personalities and social issues that are often overlooked. What an invaluable resource for students and those who care about them!

Colleen Jiron, PhD

Author's note: Jiron is the author of *Brainstorming: Using Neuropsychology in the School Setting* (2004, Western Psychological Services) and "Assessing and Intervening with Children with Externalizing Disorders," in *Best Practices in School Neuropsychology: Guidelines for Effective Practice, Assessment, and Evidence-Based Practice* (2010, Wiley & Sons).

Preface

I sat straight up in bed, awakening from a sound sleep. Peeling my eyes open, I looked at the clock—it was 4 a.m. A picture clearly emerged in my mind of the book I was meant to write. How many individualized education program (IEP) meetings had I been involved in where the child was never included with creating his or her own plan? My thoughts raced as I pondered what it must feel like to have the realization you are different from your classmates, have adults sit around a table and talk about you as if you were invisible, have paperwork shoved in front of you for your signature, and never be asked about your thoughts, feelings, what worked for you, what was frustrating, what was helpful, or what learning modality helped you grasp new concepts. How were you supposed to navigate the social scene, particularly at an older age when fitting in with one's peers matters exponentially?

As a young parent with a child who didn't hear for the first two and a half years of his life and who was also born with orthopedic issues that would require multiple surgeries, I recalled sitting in my first IEP meeting. Even though I had a bachelor's degree in elementary education, I had no idea what it meant to have a speech-language impairment. After my son was evaluated, his speech needs were explained in detail and I was told he was accepted into a preschool program for children with speech delays. Far too embarrassed to say I didn't fully understand various aspects of what I was told, I nodded in agreement and signed the papers that were thrust in front of me. I didn't really know what was said, so I blindly trusted the "educated" adults sitting across the table from me, believing that they had my son's best interests at heart.

I eventually became a special education teacher and later chaired a special education department. Prior to this, I had seen the good, the bad, and the ugly. I saw plans that were created and implemented to the letter. However, more often than I would like to acknowledge, I attended meetings where plans were created, papers were signed, and then the packet was thrown into a drawer and ignored for the rest of the year. The legal binding document that was supposed to be a guide for the student's academic or social growth was ignored or minimally implemented. I was determined this was not going to happen during my watch; everyone deserves better, especially the students entrusted to our care.

My middle-of-the-night epiphany was that while children who are two years old cannot speak for themselves, as they get older they should be included as appropriate to the point that their IEP is led by them. For example, my two-year-old son could not speak, so it was incumbent on me to advocate on his behalf. However, as he got older, he should have been asked how he liked going to see Ms. S., his speech teacher. A few years later, he should have been asked what strategies he found helpful and what he found frustrating. During his high school IEPs, he should have been able to introduce his teachers, share what he was learning in each class, and articulate what he liked about the way the teacher taught ("I find it helpful when you let my friend Joe explain math to me because he explains the steps in a way I understand") and what he found frustrating ("I feel frustrated when you discuss how we should solve for x, but you don't write it on the board").

As I was contemplating this sad state of affairs, I started to think about my son's experience. He is now an adult, and I called him to tell him about my thoughts and how it had dawned on me that I was the person I was trying to help. As I reflected on our mother-son experience, the IEP process, and the education system, I realized he had rarely spoken during the meetings. Well intentioned, I always spoke on his behalf. When I asked him what he recalled about his IEP experiences, he responded, "I think in all of my IEP meetings combined, I said maybe 100 words." My heart broke, but his words confirmed what I needed to do. It may be too late for me to turn back the clock for my own son, but there are many other parents now walking in my shoes and experiencing the same frustrations, confusion, and disappointments.

While I was serving as a special education department chair at the high school level, there were many times new students moved to our school. During the intake meeting, I would ask them what they knew about their disability. Most students had a learning disability, and their response was, "I'm stupid." When I asked them why they thought that, they frequently responded, "I had a teacher who told me," or "My friends tell me I am." Almost all of them were delightfully amazed to learn that they had an IQ within the average range. Furthermore, when queried, most students replied that they were never asked what strategies worked for them or what they believed reasonable goals were in a certain subject. I would look at their parent(s), who would concur.

As I contemplated my college education and on-the-job training, I reflected on the multitude of courses I had on my transcript and workshops I had attended. Mostly, I learned about the various disabilities, theories and best practices, methods and materials, and what the expert researchers revealed in their data as effective strategies. Rarely did anyone discuss the child with the diagnosis and what he or she *felt*. Moreover, parents were discussed only regarding why they might be reluctant to attend IEP meetings and that their signature was required. Of course, this is an oversimplification, but it captures the essence of what I learned in academia and experienced as an educator.

This brings me to today. I believe now is an incredible opportunity (and one that is long overdue) to describe the educational experience and the IEP process from the students' and parents' point of view. I would have personally been very enlightened if a student with a disability had spoken to me when I was an aspiring educator and divulged his multilayered academic and social experiences. My eyes would have been much more open and I would have been much more prepared to support this population. Of course, I always believed I was compassionate, but compassion alone does not arm one with the knowledge and skills needed to instruct and motivate struggling students who must work twice as hard as their counterparts to attain the same success.

It is important to note that many IEP teams are struggling to meet overwhelming demands of shrinking time and budget in the context of increasing paperwork and documentation. In other words, even when the IEP team is comprised of dedicated, caring, experienced professionals, the one person who really needs to be heard (the student) is often not invited to join the discussion. Thus, this book has been written to give voice to those who struggle(d) to not only survive, but also to succeed in a system that frequently overlooks their own observations, questions, ideas, and feelings.

Acknowledgments

I wish to acknowledge and dedicate this book to all the exceptional people in our world. It is an honor to know you and those who love you unconditionally. I am a more complete person because you are in my life. I have grown exponentially through your examples of courage, patience, tenacity, and joy.

I am very grateful for the unwavering devotion from my husband, Russ. He has been a resolute supporter of my pursuits and has believed in me when I have questioned the merit of our collective sacrifice to create this book.

I would like to recognize my anonymous interviewees, who met with me on blind faith. When I shared this book's purpose with them, they did not hesitate to commit their time, emphasizing the hope that their stories would enrich the lives of those who read it. It is their recollections and reflections that breathe life into this work of love.

I am most grateful to the staff at Rowman & Littlefield. A special thank you is extended to Tom Koerner and Dean Roxanis for taking time to meet with me in person. I would also like to thank Mary McMenamin and Carly Peterson for their guidance.

Faith Andreasen, PhD

Introduction

Disabled and exceptional—many people do not understand how the two can be one and the same. They think "disability" means "inability." It is surprising for many to hear that people with a learning disability have "normal" intelligence. It is even more surprising to learn that people who can't seem to focus for a reasonable length of time are capable of having IQs that are higher than average.

It is unexpected to learn that someone who is autistic can have a genius mind for calculating numbers. It doesn't occur to many that someone with an orthopedic impairment has the same physical desire to participate in sports or a romantic relationship as his or her able-bodied counterparts. Yet all these statements are true. So why does the education community so often alienate this exceptional population from academic and elective classes, sometimes by default (not acknowledging an issue needs attention) or by overreacting (excluding them from classes with their friends in the general education curriculum, believing it is an act of kindness)?

PURPOSE

Learning about students with disabilities is required of all educators, school psychologists, counselors, social workers, and other ancillary staff. Basic guidelines exist in the United States via the Individuals with Disabilities Act (IDEA), which requires that all students receive a Free and Appropriate Education (FAPE) in the Least Restrictive Environment (LRE). The United States also has a law called No Child Left Behind (NCLB), which provides standards that all students are expected to meet in order to graduate. However, the decision of how this is to occur is left to individual states. The idea of including students with disabilities in classes with their general education peers is frequently dismissed as a mild (and sometimes not so mild) inconvenience by educators who feel unfairly saddled and ill equipped to handle this responsibility. Those who are open to the idea of working with students who have "special needs" frequently need mentoring to learn how to implement best practices for this population.

Extend this issue to students in various countries and one can see quite a conundrum. Caught in the middle are the students themselves, who want to fit in without being bullied and who do not want to stand out as being "different." The fundamental purpose of this book is to inform educators about the individual student perspective regarding his or her disability by allowing educators, parents, and others to see the souls of the children whose lives they impact on a daily basis. For students, it describes their embarrassment, how they felt when bullied or called "stupid" or "lazy," and the obstacles they had to overcome. For parents, it captures their pain when they first learned their child had a disability and the fight they faced as they attempted to advocate for their child (usually not knowing their rights or appropriate strategies).

AUDIENCE

Exceptional People: Lessons Learned from Special Education Survivors is written primarily for university faculty and students in the field of education and the social sciences, current teachers, ancillary staff, administrators, and policy makers. This book is also appropriate for parents as a self-help resource. They can learn what other parents encountered within the educational environment, thus being able to better advocate for their child. High school and college students can benefit from the strategies both educators and their parents implement. Additionally, they can read portions of the book that are appropriate to their issues, realize they are not alone, and learn how to self-advocate.

APPROACH

Exceptional People is a compilation of stories from the perspectives of students who have disabilities and parents of students with disabilities. The stories are recorded without judgment or correction to the individual's perception. If only the student was interviewed and not the parent, "Tips for Teachers," "Tips for Students," and "Tips for Parents" appear at the end of the chapter. However, if the parent was interviewed, "Tips for Parents" was placed at the end of that chapter. The "Tips" list is certainly not exhaustive as there are many strategies for each situation. Although many "tips" listed are common knowledge among educators, there was an attempt to research and credit other authors who have described these strategies in their work.

ORGANIZATION

Each chapter in the text relates the story of an individual with a disability or of the parent of an individual who has a disability. Although each student's exceptionality is defined as his or her story is told, common labels are described here for your convenience. Summarized from the Texas Council for Developmental Disabilities (2008), this list speaks to what educators most often see in schools:

- Learning Disabled (LD): Among exceptional students, a learning disability describes almost 50 percent of this population. It is manifested as having difficulty within one of the following: oral expression, listening comprehension, written expression, reading skills, reading fluency, reading comprehension, math calculations, or math reasoning. Professionals or parents usually note difficulty with the student's academics, such as an inability to problem solve at the same level as his or her peers. In addition, students often experience difficulty interpreting social cues among their classmates, a difficulty that results in conflict for reasons misunderstood by the student with the disability and that triggers immense frustration.

- Speech-Language Impaired (SLI)—SLI students have difficulty understanding others and putting their own thoughts into words. This often affects their ability to correctly write a sentence by stringing together words in the correct order. It also can affect their ability to read. Among exceptional students, approximately 20 percent are described as SLI. When speaking, these students often omit sounds or parts of words (*wa* for *water*), substitute inappropriate sounds for those they struggle to form (*Bappy* for *Patty*), or distort the word (*flountain* for *fountain*). They may also have long pauses when they speak as they are attempting to put the words together in their mind before saying them audibly, have verbal blocks because the word they want to say cannot be retrieved from their brain, or they may speak very quickly, making it impossible for the listener to understand their statement. SLI students may also have apraxia (not being able to engage the correct motor movement to produce the desired speech), syntactic disorders (difficulty saying their words in the correct order), or semantic disorders (wrong word usage).

- Emotionally Disturbed or Emotional Behavioral Disorder (ED or EBD)—Among exceptional students, approximately 8 percent are described as ED or EBD. Many characteristics describe this population, including anxiety and mood disorders, obsessive-compulsive disorder (OCD), oppositional defiant disorder (ODD), and schizophrenia. Most ED students have externalizing behaviors exhibited through verbal and physical aggression. Some students, however, internalize their feelings and are extremely passive, which makes identifying them quite difficult because they tend to get lost in the crowd. To be described as ED, one must display inappropriate behaviors to a "marked degree" and over a long period of time (usually defined as six months). The student usually responds to situations in an excessive manner, for example, by fighting or swearing over a small matter, and has difficulty establishing or maintaining friendships. Most importantly, the student's behavior interferes not only with his or her learning, but also with the teacher's ability to provide an effective educational environment for other students.

- Intellectually Disabled (ID)—also referred to as *cognitive disabled* or *mentally retarded*—Among exceptional students, approximately 10 percent are described as ID. To qualify as ID, students must have an IQ of 70 or less and have limited adaptive behaviors, meaning, they have difficulty making choices, solving everyday problems, employing good judgment and insight, and setting goals for themselves. Students with mild ID can often be educated with their general education peers. They enjoy socializing and learning skills in vocational classes such as the culinary arts, pottery, automotive, and woodworking. Most ID students successfully transition to postsecondary vocations.

- Other Health Impaired (OHI)—This is the category that is most prevalent for students who have attention deficit disorder (ADD) or attention deficit hyperactivity disorder (ADHD). It also includes students who have limited strength, vitality, or alertness due to their disability or the treatment needed to address the disability. Among exceptional students, approximately 8 percent are described as OHI. As the name ADHD implies, this student displays an inability to pay attention, which is manifested by fidgeting, being easily distracted, incomplete work, excessive talking or blurting out in class, and interrupting others. Students with ADD/ADHD have difficulty processing information, consistently encoding and recalling instructions or new information due to a fluctuating ability to focus or concentrate, making decisions, solving problems, and self-regulating. About 25 percent have an anxiety disorder and about 30 percent have a reading disability.

- Multiple Disabled (MD)—Among exceptional students, approximately 2 percent are described as MD. This group includes students with severe impairments, although not exclusively. Students in this category have two or more coexisting impairments that require extensive support across many skill areas; one area of disability is nearly always in communication. Support services include speech-language training, physical therapy, occupational therapy, orientation and mobility therapy, and vision or hearing interventions. It should be noted that these students can also have average to above-average intelligence, which often may be accessible only through the use of augmentative communication devices.

- Orthopedically Impaired (OI)—Among exceptional students, approximately 1 percent are described as OI. This category includes students with congenital issues (e.g., the absence of a limb or the presence of clubfeet), disease (e.g., bone tuberculosis), and other issues such as cerebral palsy (CP), an amputation due to an accident, or bones that fracture.

- Hearing Impaired (HI)—Among exceptional students, approximately 1 percent are described as HI. This disorder is caused by genetics, a traumatic event, developmental abnormality, or infection. Sometimes the inner ear is unable to transmit a signal to the brain (sensorineural hearing loss), but sometimes there is an obstruction or damage in the middle or external portion of the ear (conductive hearing loss). Students who experience a hearing loss often understandably experience difficulty with speech and language. Additionally, they are frequently unable to experience a complete classroom educational experience that is commensurate with their peers.

- Visually Impaired (VI)—For educational purposes, visually impaired students have their learning ability impacted due to their level of functional vision. Students who are functionally blind have limited vision, so they often use their auditory (hearing) and tactile (sense of touch) abilities for learning. A student who is totally blind is completely dependent on the use of auditory and tactile channels. Fewer than 1 percent of exceptional students are described as VI.

- Autistic (A)—This neurodevelopmental disability impacts a student's ability to communicate, effectively regulate focus and attention (students become hyperfocused and distressed when their object of interest is changed or removed), and interact socially with peers. Additionally, academic performance is compromised. Although the rate of autism is contested, it is thought that among exceptional students, fewer than 1 percent

are autistic. Behaviors that are associated with autism include self-stimu-
lating movements (twirling hair, tapping a pencil, or rocking in a chair),
repetitive behaviors (arm flapping, head banging), and the desire for a
consistent schedule. Asperger's syndrome, Rett's disorder, and childhood
disintegrative disorder are included in the autism spectrum disorder (ASD)
umbrella. Students with Asperger's have social impairments but possess a
larger vocabulary than those with autism. Rett's is a progressively degen-
erative disease that affects mostly females. A student is said to have childhood disintegrative disorder when clear regression in several areas of
functioning occurs after at least two years of seemingly typical development and before age ten.

- Traumatic Brain Injury (TBI)—Students who have sustained a brain injury due to an external force that affects their educational performance meet
  the legal definition of TBI. However, schools are usually very compassionate and also label students who have had or currently have brain
  tumors as TBI. The justification is that their educational performance is
  compromised by the invasion of the tumor (and sometimes the subsequent
  surgery). TBI students can struggle in one or more of the following areas:
  speech and language, abstract thinking, reasoning, motor abilities, information processing, memory, attention, and social behavior. Less than 1
  percent of the student population meets this definition.

- Developmentally Delayed (DD)—This term applies to students aged three
  through nine who experience physical, social/emotional, communicative,
  and/or cognitive delays and therefore require special education or related
  services. No data delineates the percentage of students who qualify for
  services as DD. The goal is to identify students as early as possible so
  effective interventions can be implemented without stigmatizing the child
  with a specific label. Programs are provided to both the student and the
  family to equip the child with skills in areas that would otherwise be
  deficient.

The above list does not describe the multiple and various nuances involved
within the same exceptionality. That is, the same exceptionality can manifest
itself quite differently from student to student. For example, some learning
disabled students function well with few accommodations in the regular
education classroom while others may need extensive support. Some autistic
students participate appropriately in academic and music classes while others
are highly annoyed by the closeness of their classmates or the vibrations
caused by instruments.

As you read about various student and parent experiences, remember that the interview process, especially when it occurs years after the experience, is often recalled with varying perceptions. The full scope of details, coping mechanisms, strategies used by teachers, parental involvement, and other specifics can be forgotten, minimalized, or exaggerated due to the passage of time. With this in mind, be assured that every attempt was made to capture the interviewees' experiences as honestly as possible. Please note that all names have been changed with the exception of those of Mercedez and her mother, which have been used with permission. Any resemblance of the interviewee to someone you know is purely coincidental.

The chapters in this book can be read in any order. It is, however, more beneficial to read the stories of the child with a disability and the parent of that child together (for example, Chris and Chris's parents) to gain a more complete understanding of how they both viewed their journey. Often, their perspectives coincided rather neatly; other times, they diverged.

REFERENCE

Texas Council for Developmental Disabilities (2008). Project IDEAL: Informing and designing education for all learners. Retrieved from http://projectidealonline.org/ overview.php.

Chapter 1

Chris's Story

Emotional and Writing Exceptionality

Chris was identified as a student who needed to receive services for both an emotional and a writing disability when he was in the fourth grade. Tall for his age and very kind, he was an easy target for bullies because he internalized his feelings and would not assert himself. He elucidates that he felt extremely unhappy because he had transferred to a new school and missed his friends. Because he did not want to be in a new school, he shut down emotionally and subsequently was not performing academically.

Additionally, writing was difficult as he struggled to generate creative ideas; when he did formulate them in his mind, he strained to get them from his brain onto his paper. When he was placed into the resource environment, it was explained to him that he was going to acquire the help and attention he needed. He was satisfied with this explanation and remembers that he did considerably better in his resource classes, although his work was not completely up to the same level where it was prior to the move.

In sixth grade, Chris was moved into the general education environment, where three teachers would circulate into and out of his class. These teachers would lecture at the board but not fully explain what the parameters were for an acceptable assignment. Moreover, two of his three teachers did not circulate and assist students. After a short time, Chris was not doing well academically.

Furthermore, Chris was having trouble with a few of his peers who were constantly bullying him. The bullying matter was especially problematic because his teachers were not properly intervening on his behalf, and this made him feel they were washing their hands of the issue. He was ultimately evaluated and placed into a self-contained classroom for students who were

1

not being successful academically because their behavior was interfering with their success (in this case due to withdrawing and shutting down). When he was placed into the self-contained class, he was told that the reason was that his grades were slipping and this placement would provide the support he needed. He states, "I already knew that my counseling wasn't helping, I was withdrawn and having social problems, and so the change of placement made sense."

Chris met the teacher and the students in the self-contained classroom and liked them, so he felt good about the placement. He states, "I felt relief because I was able to get away from the peers that were bothering me—the troublemakers who were constantly harassing me. I felt the work I received in sixth grade challenged me appropriately. Mostly, I was able to focus and complete my work because I was away from the constant noise, harassment, and lack of instruction that existed in my other classroom. I was able to complete my work in a timely fashion and received decent grades." Although social skills were taught daily, Chris does not remember any specifics about what he learned.

In the seventh grade, Chris entered a new school and was placed in all general education classrooms. Eventually his teachers recognized he had some writing issues and so they placed him in resource classes for English and history. Otherwise, he took classes with his general education peers. This arrangement enabled him to get decent grades in all his classes. Chris believes he received appropriate grade-level instruction at this time but the negative experience with his agitating, bullying peers remained. The principal and counselors were apparently unaware of his social issues and that appropriate interventions existed in his individualized education program (IEP). "No teachers at this school stepped in and helped me at that time or any other time."

To avoid being confronted and bullied during lunch, Chris volunteered to work as a server in the cafeteria. Nonetheless, there occurred an incident in which his new leather jacket was taken from the place where he hung it while working. Chris assumed it was stolen; it was actually hidden from him. He angrily stormed down the hallway and physically confronted the student he thought had taken his prized possession. Both students were taken to the principal's office and full suspension was recommended.

When Chris's father arrived at the school, he was surprised to learn that the principal did not know Chris was receiving services for bullying issues such as this. His father adamantly defended him because Chris was standing up for himself over an issue that had a resounding theme—bullying. During this time of intense distress, Chris recalls that the other student's parent did not attend this conference and states, "I felt bad for him." Ultimately, the other student was placed on full suspension and Chris was placed into in-school suspension (ISS) for a week. In ISS, even though he was in attendance and completed his assignments, he did not receive credit for his work per school policy.

After this incident, Chris's parents withdrew him from the school and placed him in another school, where he experienced success through the eighth grade. He continued to receive assistance for his writing needs. He recalls that he greatly disliked his science teacher because "he did not teach, had no classroom management and was mean to the other students. Many of the students in that class did not receive passing grades." Conversely, he recalls having one specific teacher who really helped him. Chris would check in with her regularly and she ensured that his teachers were providing the accommodations he needed.

In high school, Chris was placed into all regular education classrooms again. Unfortunately, he was not given the full support he needed in English. Specifically, he was not provided the accommodation of extra time. Subsequently, he struggled with his essays because he was unable to compose them with sufficient detail, resulting in a failing grade in the course. Chris was able to take summer school in order to make up the credit.

In his tenth-grade year, Chris was placed back into a special education resource class with a teacher who clearly delineated what he wanted and how he wanted it, and explained what Chris could do in order to improve his work. "Each student received attention and my experience was good." In his senior year, Chris was once again in a regular education English class and once again began to struggle. "My teacher did not provide clear instructions and did not teach much during class time. I was therefore placed back into a resource classroom, did OK for the rest of the year, and was able to graduate on time."

Chris does not believe his peers treated him differently because he was in resource classes. "I was treated differently before being placed in resource because I was different inasmuch as I was significantly taller than my peers and nonconfrontational. Being tall made me a target for the bullies because I would not respond aggressively when they taunted me. Any little difference people see they take advantage of because they are cruel."

Chris does not recall being in any individualized education program (IEP) meetings except for his last one early in his senior year. The decision was made to place him in all general education classes, but he was not successful and was eventually placed back into resource class to support his writing. Being once again isolated from his general education peers, he was annoyed. He felt he could have passed his class, but the adults were concerned he would not pass and graduate. He was not asked how he felt about the situation and chose to keep his feelings to himself.

Chris feels the system held him back by giving him lower-level work that did not challenge him intellectually. He reasons that more teacher-student collaboration through one-on-one assistance, more specific instruction that clearly explained expectations, and after-school tutoring would have been helpful. He feels that if teachers had been willing to invest another fifteen minutes, it would have made a significant difference; instead, it was much more convenient to ignore his needs.

Chris did not have a best time of day when at school. He perceived one day as being as miserable as the one that preceded it. He does feel he connected with his high school physical education teachers and enjoyed the different activities he participated in such as basketball. "Exercise was fun while the rest of my day was just work."

He also liked his math teachers and is proud that he was one of their best students. "They explained their information, mostly on the board, and if anyone asked for clarification they gave good answers." Conversely, he believes his English teachers did not provide clear explanations to him. He concedes math is more concrete and absolute while English is more creative, requiring a certain kind of critical thinking skill, and therefore more difficult. "Each teacher appeared to have their own choice of writing styles. Changing what was learned one year to comply with a new requirement the next seemed unnecessary and irresponsible."

Chris took his course tests with his peers and had no problems except when he was expected to write creatively. Because he was very methodical and meticulous, he needed more time to complete his work. He took the state standardized test required by the No Child Left Behind Act (NCLB) with his peers and describes it as being simple and therefore not difficult for him. He does not believe taking a standardized test has value. He also feels it was "dummied down" and easy.

Upon reflection, Chris recalls two people who were the most instrumental in helping him attain educational success. First was his tenth-grade English teacher, who patiently explained what he needed in concrete terms. Second was his high school caseworker, who regularly ensured he was getting the accommodations he needed. He felt comfortable checking in with her because she would listen to him. Chris's postsecondary goal was to work with his dad. He does not recall his case manager, school psychologist, social worker, or any other person discussing course work, agencies, or organizations that could assist him with transition strategies to meet this goal.

Chris began working at his father's business "because Dad was having difficulty finding good help." He states, "I love my work," although he confesses that working with a dad who is also the boss can be tricky. He believes his dad expects more from him than he would from others and describes his teaching method as difficult to understand.

He thinks sometimes his dad explains what he wants one way when in reality he wants it done another way and that he is sometimes asked to complete a task without complete instructions. "After the task is complete, my dad then shows me what I have done wrong—after the fact." Chris asserts that some of his tasks are learned by feel and can be perfected only with time. He hopes to become a manager this year and believes this will happen "because I am very dependable."

Chris claims that the best thing about completing high school is that he does not have to "deal with those people anymore." His best experience has been having the ability to travel. He notes that traveling with others provides safety, and it means one is less likely to be scammed.

Chris's recommendation to teachers who work with students who need writing assistance is to provide concrete statements such as, "I want this sentence here, I want the ending to look like this, I want you to elaborate this way." As for teachers who work with withdrawn students, he encourages them to ask students questions to ensure each one understands the concept discussed and what is expected as an acceptable finished product. "They [the students] are too shy to ask for help themselves."

To students like him who are withdrawn, he states that he understands that fear is a monumental issue. He asserts, "You should learn to ignore your fear and the anticipated judgment you think you will face. Get up and say what you really want to say, and then hope for the best. It might not work out, but it might. Take the chance and speak up." Chris does believe he speaks up more now and surmises he has learned to do so because his current job requires him to interact frequently with customers. For this, he is thankful.

TIPS FOR TEACHERS OF EMOTIONALLY WITHDRAWN STUDENTS

- Learn the student's history.
- Provide predictable, fair, firm parameters.
- Enforce firm rules that are clearly delineated.
- Actively listen.
- Offer positive reinforcement.
- Adapt instruction to the student's needs.
- Offer the student assistance frequently.
- Model appropriate interactions.
- Encourage communication.
- Recognize needs through facial expressions or inactivity.

- Stop talking and briefly withdraw if you see the student becoming upset, then approach to query.
- Practice social skill strategies regularly.
- Teach problem-solving skills, such as how to compromise.
- Provide the student with scheduled or provisional (such as with a "Freedom Ticket") intervals of quiet and/or solitude.
- Intervene early to prevent a simple problem from becoming a serious one.
- Embed antibullying practices into an existing schoolwide positive behavior support system.
- Set firm limits regarding acceptable behavior.
- Monitor progress and adjust instruction or social interactions accordingly.

TIPS FOR TEACHERS OF STUDENTS WITH WRITING EXCEPTIONALITIES

- Develop pre-skills and background knowledge, discuss, model, memorize, provide guided practice, provide independent practice.
- Help students implement POW: Pick my ideas, Organize my notes, Write and say more.
- Build on POW by reviewing TREE: Topic Sentence, Reasons—three or more, Examine, Ending.
- Offer a pencil grip as needed.
- Afford opportunities to use different writing instruments and paper.
- Provide clear criteria and explicit examples.
- Teach proofreading techniques.
- Analyze spoken language to determine if it is proficient; if not, consider further evaluation for speech issues.
- Ask open-ended questions to prompt students' thought processes.
- Assign shorter tasks and analyze their quality before requiring longer ones.
- Check work frequently as the student is working.
- Encourage the student to read his work aloud to self-check its quality.
- Provide a note card for reference regarding the student's writing issue, for example, noun-verb agreements, incomplete thoughts, the lack of supporting sentences.
- Practice combining short sentences to create ones that are complex.
- Practice functional writing, for example, completing job applications, writing checks, creating résumés.
- Provide an accommodation of additional time to complete written work.
- Permit the use of a computer for assignments.
- Allow the student to write about a topic of interest.

- Reduce distracting stimuli.
- Teach the five Ws.
- Avoid interruption if the student is engaged in a writing activity.
- Praise the student for effort.
- Provide evaluative feedback that is instructional.
- Teach students to plan, write, and revise.
- Ensure that one style of writing is mastered before introducing another style.
- Provide think sheets or mnemonics.
- Modify assignments as appropriate.
- Coordinate writing instruction with the efforts of an occupational therapist.

TIPS FOR STUDENTS WHO ARE EMOTIONALLY WITHDRAWN

- Practice relaxation such as deep breathing or yoga.
- Eat well.
- Exercise so every cell has oxygen.
- Talk to someone you trust.
- Practice thinking positive thoughts.
- Rehearse conversation starters with people you know, for example, "Hi, I'm Chris," or "That jacket looks great."
- Write down and rehearse things you could say in a conversation before you engage in it.
- Encourage yourself to try—join a group activity you would enjoy, for example, chess, basketball.
- Develop assertive behavior, for example, telling someone what you enjoy or your choice in where to go.

TIPS FOR STUDENTS WITH WRITING EXCEPTIONALITIES

- Don't try to write straight from your head.
- Write everything down—this makes your ideas more concrete.
- Begin by brainstorming ideas, then review your list to see which ideas relate to each other.
- If lists aren't helpful, try free-writing to get your ideas.
- Develop a thesis statement—it's okay if it starts out convoluted.
- Create an outline to organize ideas.
- Use a tape recorder if talking is easier than writing—transcribe your ideas later.

- Read your paper out loud to "hear" if it seems orderly.
- Use colored note cards, markers, and highlighters to organize ideas.

REFERENCES

Farley, A. (2011, August 24). Teaching strategies for emotionally disturbed students. *eHow Family*. Retrieved from http://www.ehow.com/info_12003377_teaching-strategies-emotion-ally-disturbed-students.html.

Gersten, R., Baker, S., & Edwards, L. (1999, May). Effective teaching practices. *Keys to successful learning summit*. Symposium conducted at the meeting of the National Center for Learning Disabilities in partnership with the Office of Special Education Programs and the National Institute of Child Health & Human Development, Washington, DC.

Gocsik, K. (2006, October 18). Learning disabilities. *Dartmouth Writing Program*. Retrieved from http://www.dartmouth.edu/~writing/materials/student/special/disabilities.shtml.

Good, C. P., McIntosh, K., & Gietz, C. (2011, September/October). Integrating bullying prevention into schoolwide positive behavior support. *Teaching Exceptional Children, 44*(1), 48–56.

Graham, S. (2010, September). Want to improve children's writing? Don't neglect their handwriting. *Educational Digest, 76*(1), 49–55.

Lyness, D. (2010, October). Anxiety disorders. *TeensHealth*. Retrieved from http://kidshealth.org/teen/your_mind/mental_health/anxiety.html?tracking=T_RelatedArticle#.

———. (2010, August). Social phobia. *TeensHealth*. Retrieved from http://kidshealth.org/teen/your_mind/mental_health/so-cial_phobia.html?tracking=T_RelatedArticle#a_What_Is_Social_Phobia_.

———. (2010, August). 5 ways to shake shyness. *TeensHealth*. Retrieved from http://kid-shealth.org/teen/your_mind/emotions/shy_tips.html?tracking=T_RelatedArticle.

Mason, L. H., Kubina, R., & Taft, R. J. (2011, February). Developing quick writing skills of middle school students with disabilities. *Journal of Special Education, 44*(4), 205–220.

Solar, E. (2011, September/October). Prove them wrong: Be there for secondary students with an emotional or behavioral disability. *Teaching Exceptional Children, 44*(1), 40–45.

Chapter 2

Chris's Parents' Story

Emotional and Writing Exceptionality

Chris was first identified as needing exceptional student services for emotional and writing support when he was in the fourth grade. His parents sadly recall that he was having difficulty socially after he was transferred into a new school; he became extremely withdrawn and had no friends. Furthermore, difficulty in writing was first noted by his math teacher because he would only record his answers and not show his work.

Later, Chris's English teacher shared that Chris was having difficulty recording his thoughts and editing his papers, and would not complete his work. Mother states he was a perfectionist and would focus on quality rather than quantity, "which bothered some of his teachers." The issue was that he could not produce the same amount of writing as his peers given the same amount of time to complete his work. He had to write very deliberately and meticulously when he worked on his assignments. When Chris was initially identified as a student with a writing disability, his parents thought there would be a short period of interventions and then he would be able to progress with no difficulties; this clearly was not the case.

The first serious behavioral incident Chris's parents recall occurred during his fourth-grade year. The teacher was conducting a group activity during which Chris was made fun of because he was so much taller than his classmates. He got extremely angry and, for the first time ever, responded physically by punching the taunting student. Chris was decisively disciplined, but as a result of that incident, school personnel were concerned minor occurrences would result in his reacting violently.

Chris continued through the fifth grade in the same school. A family friend told his parents that she would walk by Chris's room and see him with his head on his desk and his arms over his head because the students were acting out and the teacher was not in the room. Chris was shut down and would not participate, not wanting to be part of the chaos. As a result, his classmates would bully him. His being targeted by bullies was eventually noted by school personnel. His parents lament, "He was always so much physically larger than children his own age that his passive nature made him an easy target for his peers."

Chris entered the sixth grade in a different school and was placed in the general education classroom for all classes with no support in spite of what was delineated in his individualized education program (IEP). Again, there was a problem with his math teacher because Chris would not write the steps to show how he arrived at his answer. His parents assert that he could easily calculate numbers in his head and therefore viewed writing, a skill with which he struggled, as an unnecessary waste of time.

The initial conversation with Chris's teacher regarding this matter occurred when his parents saw that he was emotionally shutting down over the matter, which they feared meant he would stop doing work in any of his courses. The response from the sixth-grade teacher was that he needed to see more writing from Chris showing how he arrived at his answers. Father asked the teacher if the answers provided were correct. The teacher responded that they were but avowed he still wanted to see Chris's thought process on paper. Father inquired whether it was more important that his son was able to accurately arrive at the correct answer or if it was more important for him to do unnecessary writing that Chris found to be laborious.

The teacher explained that sometimes Chris would arrive at an answer by using a process different from what was modeled in the textbook and this troubled the teacher. Father retorted that he thought this ability demonstrated great skill on his son's part. The teacher remained firmly resolved that not solving problems by following the book's example illustrated Chris's unwillingness to comply with requests. This started an argument regarding Chris's intelligence that led Father to request a complete battery of tests by the school psychologist. Test results ranked his math IQ at 147. (Later in high school, he tested in the top 3 percent in math in the nation and later tutored a couple of students in math—those students grasped the concepts and understood the content due to his resourceful mentoring skills.)

Socially, there were a few classmates who unrelentingly bullied Chris, yet his teachers "would turn a blind eye." Father went to the school and emphatically said, "Evidently, we have a problem, and I would like to know what those of you who work within the school system are going to do." (He defined the problem as Chris's being bullied.)

The sixth-grade teacher had no response, so Chris's parents brought the matter to the principal. A meeting was held and the school psychologist and team determined that receiving support in the self-contained behavior intervention classroom would be an appropriate placement. The goal was to remove Chris from his current ineffectual environment. This would permit him to regain his self-worth by benefiting from a classroom where he could work without the distraction of being bullied, with frequent teacher assistance, and with an excellent social skills program that would help him learn how to be assertive rather than passive. Subsequently, Chris received grade-level work and participated in a nationally recognized social skills curriculum. After Chris was placed in the self-contained classroom, his parents perceived he was happier as he was receiving extra attention and was not getting teased.

When Chris entered the seventh grade, he went yet again to another school. He became less happy because he was placed in all general education classes with no support and he was once again being bullied. One positive aspect of his day was band, a class he took on the recommendation of the school psychologist, who was attempting to place him in social situations; she surmised music would be easy because it correlates with math. He played the tuba (although it was not his preferred instrument) and did it quite well due to the instruction and mentoring of his band teacher. He was so good that he occasionally was invited to play with the high school band. "One could say he enjoyed the experience in spite of himself. However, he did not pursue band when he left the school."

While in seventh grade, to avoid his peers, Chris volunteered to work in the cafeteria. The positive aspect is that this gave him self-esteem; he received payment and was able to eat for free. However, his parents recognized this for what it was—a ploy to avoid social situations and confrontations.

Father and Mother sadly recall a specific incident in which Chris's cherished leather coat was taken during lunch; it was actually hidden from him but he thought it was stolen because it was not where he left it. The student who did this thought it was "funny." Chris physically confronted the student and they both ended up in the principal's office.

When Father arrived at the school, he discovered that the principal was unaware Chris was a student who received services and that specific guidelines for such situations were delineated in his IEP. Those guidelines said that if Chris was ever in an altercation he was to be removed from that situation, the school psychologist was to be contacted, his counselor was to be called, and his parents were to be called immediately. Father recalls, "That never happened because the vice principal at that school did not even know Chris was a special needs child; subsequently, he fell through the crack again. After the principal had already started a disciplinary confrontation with Chris and made him feel worse than he already felt, they called me. They were going to expel him and send him across the street to an alternative placement."

Upon learning what happened, Father asked the principal, "Do you have any idea who this kid is?" and the principal did not. Father was greatly disheartened as he believes the school principal's first responsibility is to identify whether a student is receiving services for special needs or not. "Had he done his job he would have been able to keep a closer eye on Chris and situations that he encountered, thus helping him as each issue arose. I was also upset when I found out the counselor did nothing to assist Chris in this situation. The counselor washed his hands of the matter by stating Chris had never been in his office before so he saw no reason to be concerned about him." Father asked the counselor who the adult was and therefore who needed to take some responsibility and be proactive.

After much heated discussion, the school psychologist was contacted; she went to the school and shared information from Chris's IEP. She explained that he should not be around aggressive students and full suspension was not appropriate. School officials then realized that nothing that was in his IEP had been implemented up to that point in the school year.

The final decision was to place Chris in in-school suspension (ISS) so he would understand that fighting was not an appropriate solution to resolve problems. It was explained that he should receive this consequence so that all the students in the school understood that "if you choose to fight you are going to be held accountable." Chris's parents explained to him that even though the other student did not behave appropriately, it was not OK to fight; they acknowledge that their son was guilty of throwing the first punch. His parents also explained that he had a right to defend himself but that he could not start a fight. "In this situation, the other student meant no harm; he just thought he was being funny. Conversely, all Chris really wanted was to be left alone. The response from the school was immediate and devastating to our son as he had finally stood up for himself only to be knocked to the ground by adults via the insolent tone with which he was chastised."

Following this incident, an IEP meeting was held to determine strategies to help Chris come out of his shell appropriately; his parents recall that the school counselor was absent from this meeting, and they considered this unprofessional. Ultimately, the only support Chris was going to receive was for writing in a resource English class. Subsequently, his parents moved him to another school for the remainder of his seventh-grade and all of his eighth-grade year. "He received a great counselor in his new school that latched onto him and ensured he received the support he needed. She would have him check in with her fifteen minutes prior to the start of the school day once a week. He looked forward to this and enjoyed having a trusted contact person."

At this time, Chris's writing issues were more heavily targeted and support was more clearly spelled out in greater detail. In this new junior high school Chris had the accommodation of extra time to complete his assignments. This helped him with his writing and thought processes. "His counselor followed through with every teacher every year and they all knew what was expected, what was allowable, and what his accommodations were. She even had the foresight to invite his future high school counselor to his eighth-grade IEP meeting to ensure his transition would go smoothly."

Because his junior high school counselor was so proactive, when Chris entered high school he was set up for success as appropriate school personnel knew he was a student who received services. Thus, his ninth- and tenth-grade years were quite successful although he continued to struggle with English and was continually bullied. Regarding writing, transferring his thoughts from his head to paper became more challenging each year as he progressed from having to complete a sentence by writing the correct verb or noun in junior high to having to create his own essays. Eventually, he had to write creatively and succinctly via argumentative essays and compare-and-contrast essays, while implementing different styles of writing. Recounting details was extremely arduous, complicated by Chris's penchant for being very methodical. Thus, what took his classmates one class period to complete might take him two or three.

Chris's writing problems were particularly difficult during his junior and senior years. His senior English teacher eventually laid out a specific program to ensure he would be able to graduate. "Chris could always read well; the problem was getting his thoughts onto paper. Even when he would verbalize his answers he had problems expressing himself and orally capturing the thoughts that were in his head. Clearly, his biggest academic problem in the school system was his English class."

To assist him with confronting bullies, the school's football coaches encouraged him to join the team, but he was not interested because he was afraid he would hurt someone. He expressed this concern to his father, who told him he was very mature to show such concern for his peers. Father therefore stepped in and asked the coaches to stop pursuing the recruitment of his son for sports.

Another issue involved military recruiters who targeted him when he was in JROTC (Junior Reserve Officers' Training Corps) in ninth and tenth grades. They constantly pursued him and made constant calls to his home. Father finally intervened and told the recruiters the calls had to stop. They responded by saying Chris was eighteen years old and could make his own choice. Father restated that they were to cease and desist. (Chris did express some interest in the Coast Guard but was too tall to qualify.)

Mother believes schools are finally starting to sit up and pay attention to a problem she complained about from the beginning of Chris's negative experience with his peers: bullying. Her complaints got progressively louder as he moved through the education system. Teachers seemed to dismiss this serious issue by brushing her concerns aside with lackadaisical statements such as, "Everyone gets bullied," or "Well, I will keep an eye out and see what I can do." Mother also feels as if she was ignored when she brought issues to the attention of school administrators. "I can only imagine what it would have been like for Chris if he had gone in and complained himself." She opines, "The level of bullying that occurs today exceeds those of yesteryear as evidenced by the zero tolerance policy that now exists on most campuses."

Mother contends that since Chris has graduated, there have been several shootings nationwide committed by students with one characteristic in common: they were bullied. She speculates that this is because teachers ignored the seriousness of the situation and acted as if it were insignificant. "The issue was Chris was not the only student being bullied, and yet teachers and administrators were choosing to ignore the issue. Today, it is like these kids want to destroy each other. They are willing to take a broken bottle to one's face." Mother always gave Chris permission to defend himself because she wanted him to understand he was valuable as a person and could stand up for himself without being punished. She is irritated that staff members at his high school expected him to run if accosted and would not permit him to defend himself.

Chris's parents recall various IEP meetings throughout his schooling that various teachers, ancillary staff, or administrators did not attend (Father recalls that educators were shocked when he showed up to an IEP meeting because fathers so rarely attended).They appreciate the fact that teachers are busy but believe attending these IEP meetings is part of their professional responsibility. "Their absence sends a negative message to the parents and to the children they serve by indicating that student issues are not important enough to devote their time to them. In fact, in high school there were times the person who was supposed to run the meeting did not show up so somebody else would step in and run the meeting. It showed a complete lack of consideration for the education system and their job." This was very unsettling.

Father believes that "if there was a required program that taught educators and ancillary staff to be as responsible as they were asking the students to be, that would be progress. It seems the acting parties that are supposed to be involved in this so-called special education system are demonstrating the child really is not that 'special.' If these adults changed their behavior and attended the meetings, maybe the child would step up because they would perceive that they really are important. When students see the adults who are supposed to care about them not make the effort to attend their meeting, they are not stupid—they get that when they are 'special needs students,' then they are not 'special' as people."

During IEP meetings Chris's parents would ask him directly what he thought about the issue being discussed, but he rarely spoke up. They speculate he believed the school personnel were going to do whatever they wanted to and there was no point in expressing his opinion. His parents tried to explain that what they were doing was trying to help him. They knew he did not like these meetings, but his parents believed they didn't have an option regarding how to help him. "His whole demeanor of not wanting to be confrontational and not wanting to argue or say something he had to back up or prove caused him to default to his withdrawal theme."

If his parents asked him what he wanted, Chris would respond that he did not know. If they asked him how he felt about being in a particular classroom, he would say he guessed it was OK. His answers were always very short. "He never said he did not want to do something that was suggested even though he may have felt it."

Chris's parents believe he had some teachers who were instrumental in helping him through school. One was his sixth-grade self-contained teacher; another was his counselor in his second junior high school. One specific strategy they thought was helpful was the requirement for Chris to meet with his counselor on a regular basis; making it his responsibility to do so gave him a sense of self-worth. "He was praised, found it enjoyable, received a sense of self-worth, and it was probably the most motivating thing that ever happened to Chris. It empowered him. It was something he was not put down for, he was not bullied for, he wasn't expected to shut up and take it; he was simply asked to perform a task and when he did it he was praised."

Conversely, the least motivating event for Chris was being punished for things he did not think were wrong. An issue perceived negatively by his parents was the time it took to consistently provide the services Chris needed. "It took a couple years to get everything into place, and then his services were sporadic, resulting in the need to constantly revisit them." They view this as a breakdown in the system.

Chris was so quiet that it was easy to not realize he had serious socioemotional and writing issues. Yet, from his parents' perspective, it appeared his teachers were willing to ignore his needs and let him slide through because that would require no effort on their part.

Father and Mother passionately believe the labels required by the federal government are not empathetic and disregard the students' and parents' feelings. At the time Chris was in school, "the terminology used for his socioemotional needs was 'severely emotionally disturbed.' We viewed this term as extremely degrading, feeling it implied he was a crazy man about to do great destruction." In his high school IEP meetings, Chris's parents could feel him cringe every time the term was said out loud. When they protested this label, school personnel replied they had to label him in order for him to receive services, and they had no choice in what the federally mandated term was. Mother states that any layman would think the term extreme, and she found it revolting. "Furthermore, the label sticks with the student for life and has a negative psychological impact."

Chris's parents say that the best time of day for him was when he got to leave school and "get away from those other kids. He was able to have some relief from those who were bullying him." Upon reflection, they note that he never came home and volunteered information regarding what he did in school during the day. "Everything had to be pried out of him. He would never openly talk to us and share what he did or what happened to him."

Regarding the transition from high school to the postsecondary world, there was no assistance from the special education department that helped Chris by informing him of available programs or organizations that could support him. Mother wanted Chris to go to college to be a certified public accountant (CPA). He liked the idea and thought accounting would be easy because it involved numbers. However, accounting is more abstract than simply solving algebraic problems, so he struggled and received a D in the course.

Chris also failed English, a course he clearly found distasteful. Mother then encouraged him to consider becoming a fireman. Chris took and passed the written test but did not pass the physical test because he was meticulous and misunderstood he was being timed. He did not go back and retest but chose to work with his father instead.

Mother states that educators need to understand that certain students do not have the ability to freely regulate their thinking. Teachers should consider that for students like Chris, the world is seen as black-and-white; it is difficult to step out of their box. Therefore, when one teacher requires a student to write in the Jane Schaffer style and another teacher changes to a different writing style, students like Chris struggle immensely. Furthermore, writing is an objective process; teachers should be thoughtful of individuals and their abilities when reviewing their work.

Mother thinks schools need to have mandatory classes that focus on life skills and trades. Examples that are currently appropriate include learning how to complete applications, write résumés, dress for interviews, balance checkbooks, welding, woodworking, culinary arts, and computer classes. She also believes placing students in a real-world work environment where they can engage in actual life experiences would be invaluable. She wishes she had required Chris to get a job at McDonald's because their world-renowned structured regimen would be helpful for someone withdrawn like him. "The environment would have been nonthreatening while exposing him to various social situations." Father interjects that he had Chris complete applications for a part-time job on the weekends in an attempt to get him around more people. However, he never got hired for any of these positions.

At twenty-two years of age, Chris was still living at home. His father forced him to make a decision regarding what he wanted besides working and hanging out in his room. Chris stated he would like to have his own place but he didn't know how to accomplish this goal. His parents helped him find and purchase property, put in utilities, pour the foundation, and place his home on it. When problems arose, Father made Chris deal with the appropriate person to rectify the situation. Mother states that he is responsible with money, as evidenced by his balanced checkbook and paid bills. They state that home ownership is the best thing that has happened to him since high school.

Father worries that Chris does not understand that his world will not always exist in its current form. For example, what will he do when they, his parents, are not available to assist with various situations? In their minds, it was expected that by the time he was twenty-five, Chris would grow out of his shyness, but this has not happened.

Father wonders if he has done Chris any favors by hiring him at his shop or if he has contributed to isolating him by giving him a safe place to withdraw. He recognizes that Chris is learning a trade but worries that he has no backup plan. He is a dependable employee and his father hopes he can take over the business one day, but Father is profoundly concerned that he quietly goes through the motions of accomplishing his responsibilities in order to avoid confrontation. Father also wonders what Chris would do if this job were not available. He does try to send him out on errands so that he has to interact with customers. Clients remark about how much they enjoy working with him and state that he is very polite, always saying "please" and "thank you." Thus, although the environment is safe, this could be positively facilitating his emotional growth by slowly integrating him into the social aspect of the business world.

Since the time he began working in his father's shop, Chris has never verbalized a desire to do anything else. Father acknowledges that if Chris really wanted to pursue another career, he would express these desires to his father. He feels confused about how to help Chris with his social issues. Chris is very intelligent and grounded, and far ahead of many of his peers as he has a good, steady job and is buying his own house; but he needs a true friend. "Part of the problem is many of the people his age do not have the same interests, are messed up in some fashion, and have the opinion that 'It's all about me.'"

Chris feels very frustrated and disappointed when peers say they will meet him but don't. In fact, it is very devastating for him. "People tend to take advantage of his good nature and then ignore him. Being taken advantage of has been Chris's most negative experience since leaving high school." His father is trying to teach him how to take charge of his life and mitigate being taken advantage of through business learning experiences.

Father states that Chris needs an excessive amount of time to process information while at work. This is detrimental when it concerns safety issues. "Chris is constantly putting himself between a rock and a hard place. He has repeatedly been told how to safely operate within the confines of the shop. Even though he understands pain, he does not believe a serious incident will happen on the job." Father posits that this is because Chris thinks he would react fast enough and is strong.

Father tries to emphasize there can be some serious consequences if Chris is not constantly aware of his surroundings and consistently implementing safety procedures. He is not sure Chris grasps the seriousness of potentially dangerous situations. For example, there was an incident in which a ten-ton truck fell on Father's head; it happened so quickly he had no time to move out of the way. While Chris stood cemented to the floor in disbelief, his other son responded quickly, so Father was okay. Father surmises that Chris reacts slowly because it takes time for him to process information, just as it took time for him to process and write information when he was in school.

Father affirms there are facets of the job that are difficult for Chris to grasp because he thinks so concretely. He likes to perform tasks the same way every time without deviating. Failure to adjust his approach to various situations is detrimental to the business. Much work has had to be redone due to his inability to think outside the box. Additionally, Chris's slow, methodical working pace puts them behind the clock, causing customers to have to wait. Even though Chris is aware of this, he has difficulty increasing his work speed.

Father states that Chris recognizes he is different and that he is not happy about that fact. Father encourages him to join activities and notes he has just joined a gym. Otherwise, Chris thinks others view him as a freak and therefore avoids pursuing outside interests. As a result, Father has suggested changes such as not dressing in black or hiding behind his sunglasses. He thinks Chris might feel people need to just accept him the way he is or not at all. "Beyond that, it is hard to know what Chris is really thinking."

Chris's parents note that society expects certain behaviors from individuals based on their looks. Because Chris is big, they expect him to be emotionally mature. Conversely, if someone is physically handicapped, society thinks he or she is also mentally handicapped. "Tall people are expected to act older than their age."

Chris's parents offer advice to other parents who have a child like him: "Fight for your child's rights and needs, have your child get a part-time job that is nonthreatening but provides an opportunity to socialize in short bursts, and don't let them fall into the deep holes they dig for themselves. Recognize that to the child, withdrawal and avoidance feels like self-survival. Therefore, give them permission to decompress through withdrawal but don't allow them to stay withdrawn."

Regarding the school system, they caution parents not to naively trust what just one person says: "The more professionals you can get involved, the better. Ask for special testing, psychologists, various teachers, and others that you know will support your child. If there is a bullying situation, recognize it can be very dangerous and notify the appropriate authorities. If you don't understand the language being used in IEP meetings, ask. If derogatory words are being used, ask the professionals to refrain from using them. If you don't feel comfortable with what is being offered, reach outside the school to obtain assistance. Don't accept that whatever the school offers is the only resource available."

Chris's parents believe all educators should be required to receive training regarding exceptional student resources that exist outside the education system. They further believe it should be mandated that these agencies are disclosed during the IEP meeting as a viable extension to one's educational programming. To parents, they suggest that they "have an alternative solution, have a backup plan, and have a way to expand your child's services. Accommodations offered through the public school system are not the only answer." They wish they had been aware of options that surely must have existed when their son was in school. In spite of not knowing about them, they believe Chris is a success story and are very proud of him.

TIPS FOR PARENTS OF STUDENTS WITH EMOTIONAL EXCEPTIONALITIES

- Provide emotional support by ensuring that your child knows you care about him or her.
- Seek opportunities for your child to interact with adults outside the family such as relatives and teachers.
- Listen to and value your child's ideas.
- Treat your child with respect by offering assistance when he or she seeks your advice.
- Seek support through training as needed, especially regarding communication.
- Make requests clear, for example, "Put *your clothes* in the drawer," instead of "Put *them* away."
- Praise your child or provide attention when a desirable behavior has occurred.
- Be consistent with your rules and the consequences for breaking them.

- State requests in positive terms such as, "I like it when you meet me on time" instead of saying, "Why are you always late?"

TIPS FOR PARENTS OF STUDENTS WITH WRITING EXCEPTIONALITIES

- Encourage your child to write lists of chores or wishes.
- Place notes in your child's lunch box or coat pocket wishing him or her a good day.
- Use a kitchen bulletin board to post notes.
- Have your child journal or write in a diary, recording significant events of the day.
- Communicate with a dialogue journal, that is, the child asks a question and the parent responds.
- Utilize current electronic communication tools to write letters to family members or friends.
- Create a Special Day Book in which various family members and friends record why your child is special.
- Play a Quick Write game—your child writes for ten minutes from your prompt, for example, "Discuss if you think soft drinks should be sold in schools," or "Describe the fun you had at your friend's pool party." Converse about the story without commenting on punctuation.
- Make "play" writing fun; avoid correcting spelling or punctuation.
- Play language games to enrich your child's vocabulary.

REFERENCES

Lavigne, J. V., LeBailly, S. A, Gouze, K. R., Binnis, H. J., Keller, J., & Pate, L. (2010, June). Predictors and correlates of completing behavioral parent training for the treatment of oppositional defiant disorder in pediatric primary care. *Behavior Therapy, 41*(2), 198–211.

Mason, L. H., Kubina, R., & Taft, R. J. (2011, February). Developing quick writing skills of middle school students with disabilities. *Journal of Special Education, 44*(4), 205–220.

Rasinski, T., & Padak, N. (2011, November 9). Write soon! *Reading Teacher, 62*(7), 618–620.

Yeung, R., & Leadbeater, B. (2009, December 16). Adults make a difference: The protective effects of parent and teacher emotional support on emotional and behavioral problems of peer-victimized adolescents. *Journal of Community Psychology, 38*(1), 80–98.

Chapter 3

Clark's Story

Spastic Diplegia Cerebral Palsy

Clark is a gregarious young man who was born with spastic diplegia, a form of cerebral palsy that affects the lower half of his body. Specifically, his lower extremities are primarily affected, as demonstrated by tight hamstrings and the lack of good balance or endurance. He has minor fine-motor issues that are apparent mainly when he writes. In his earlier years of school he needed to use a reverse walker to navigate; he began using a wheelchair in sixth grade, which helped immensely as he moved from class to class.

Clark currently prefers to ambulate in his wheelchair while home due to his lack of balance. In the workplace or at his university, he prefers to stay in his chair, as he believes that makes others more comfortable. He does physically transfer to another chair at times. He is currently not on any medications to relax his muscles.

Clark has had several surgeries throughout the years to counteract the effects of cerebral palsy. These include hamstring releases, hip muscle releases, and knee staples. He also had selective dorsal rhizotomy at the age of twelve; this is a neurosurgery that targets the rootlets of overfiring nerves. The surgery helped, but he does not believe the long-term effects have been as pronounced as when the surgery initially occurred.

Mother's labor was so difficult that the doctors were not sure her son was going to live. In the ensuing years, Clark had developmental delays, such as learning to roll over and sit up; he did not walk until he was six years old. Because he did not meet expected developmental milestones, Clark received physical and occupational therapy at an infant development center. He remembers having a good time and believes he received appropriate support. Unfortunately, the positive experiences at the center did not transfer smoothly to the public school environment.

When Clark entered kindergarten in the public school system, he remembers feeling as if he was a spectacle, standing out from his classmates. He was mainstreamed during his early years, meaning that he received instruction with his general education peers but underwent physical and occupational therapy in a separate room. His teachers and ancillary staff did not consistently communicate with his parents, and this resulted in numerous altercations with administrators. Clark feels his parents attempted to shield him from the disputes they were having with school personnel.

One of the early details Clark remembers while in kindergarten was that they gave him an IQ test to determine his educational placement. He took the test and then his parents were told he had cheated on it. His parents asked what made them think their son had cheated, and they were told he scored too high—that is, too high for a student with cerebral palsy. His parents said that they did not agree and believed he needed to be retested. When he was retested by the psychologist, the score actually went up. "This is indicative of the experience of cerebral palsy students within the educational environment; many educators cannot wrap their head around the idea that this disability does not mean one is stupid."

Clark remembers a story that his mother told him. She went to the special education director of the district to talk to him regarding appropriate strategies to support Clark's needs. The director said he had "dealt with these kinds of people before" and proceeded to physically imitate what cerebral palsy looked like using demeaning gestures such as curling his hands and helplessly flapping them. Needless to say, that was the beginning of a very rocky relationship with Mother.

Like many children and teenagers, Clark admits he was never as interested in physical therapy as he should have been, not realizing the potential benefits. He believes that if he had taken a greater interest and had more actively participated, he might have gained a more lasting benefit with better long-term results. Because his muscles did relax due to his surgery, he does not know if the resurgence of his issues is a result of his lack of interest in physical therapy or if his current condition is a result of the twenty-one years that have since elapsed, including growing and gaining weight (but not to the extent of being overweight). Clark has amblyopia (lazy eye) and wears glasses for nearsightedness, a common issue for individuals with cerebral palsy. He has no problem producing language or making decisions, and he has never needed a language board—he can type fifty-five words per minute.

Clark describes his ability to remember as good. Although he doesn't remember historical content as well as other information, if he is given a book with a story, he can remember everything verbatim. Math class is the exception to his otherwise outstanding abilities. In school, he struggled to remember his times tables and had difficulty completing timed tests.

On the other hand, if he had the option to take additional time to complete his test, he could do so and receive a decent grade. However, Clark was proud and often refused any accommodations. He believed it was just one more thing that would make him look different. When working on a whole-class activity of times tables, he could not go fast enough. Mother thinks that is the reason he hates math today.

Clark is not sure at what age he understood what his disability meant. He always knew he was different. He recalls the time he went to Disney World when he was about six years old and his parents parked in the handicapped area. One of the parking attendants told his parents they couldn't park there because it was handicapped parking. Clark spoke up and asked the attendant, "What do you think I am? I wouldn't be this size if I wasn't handicapped." The attendant was quite embarrassed. So Clark realized he had a disability although he did not fully understand it.

Clark participated in wheelchair basketball from age seven to seventeen. Others in this group had spinal cord injuries or spina bifida. That activity helped him get comfortable when interacting with those around him and helped him realize he had a place in society. Although he confesses he was not the best player, his participation helped him get comfortable with ambulating in his chair. Clark stresses that this organization was instrumental in giving him a sense that the life he was living could work. Now, years later, he still feels a connection with the wheelchair basketball community.

As he was going through school, his level of involvement in classroom activities depended on the school, teacher, and activity. He did not initially feel stupid and was always gregarious, which helped him. However, one painful incident of exclusion occurred when his class went on a field trip to a park that was not accessible to him. He was given the choice to have his mother pick him up so he could go home, stay at school, or go to the ranger's shack at the park and watch movies. He chose the shack; a friend opted to stay with him. The overall sense was that his teachers did not seem to care that he was left out; their actions conveyed that it was more important to give the "normal" students a memorable experience and exclude him than it was to schedule a field trip where he could be included.

Clark was left to figure out how to internally resolve these painful matters himself. He describes this as a "weird recurring theme." He states that he has not necessarily dwelled on grieving over these painful moments in his heart but now recognizes he was often given a subtle, and sometimes not so subtle, indication that he and his parents were going to have to learn to deal with this issue of exclusion throughout his life. "The message was that we needed to accept the fact that I was never going to be a part of what was going on around me."

Clark had an annual individualized education program (IEP) meeting throughout his public school years. Either the school psychologist or the physical therapist ran the meeting. His disability was described to him as brain damage—his brain is sending more signals than it should to his legs. In later years, enrichment was part of his education. His IQ is about 130, so he was placed in the gifted program. This was a separate class he was in from fifth through eighth grade.

Clark wonders why this "enrichment" time of day was not used to learn more useful skills. He remembers doing some activities that were more mechanical in nature, some were more theatrical, and some were timed. He remembers this as fun, but not necessarily worthwhile in the sense that, over the years, he has found that he does not use anything that he did in that class. The positive aspect is that he was around similarly minded students who had stimulating conversations, making it a more comfortable place to be compared to his regular classes. There was a lot of individuality going on and a lot of similarities among those in the class, so he did not stand out as much as he did in his regular classroom.

Clark recalls that his parents were included in his (IEP) meetings—Mom would have insisted. In elementary school, he remembers multiple carbon copies existed, but Mom spoke in his behalf until approximately junior high school. He believes the adults said something like, "Is that all right with you?" and he nodded in agreement, papers were passed around and signed, and the meeting was adjourned. Clark grew more comfortable with giving input during IEP meetings as he grew older. For example, in high school he requested Advanced Placement classes (AP) and they were scheduled for him.

Clark believes his IEP goals were implemented, not merely written on paper; however, implementation was not necessarily effective. For example, when he was in elementary school, he was strapped into a device that kept him vertical in a desk up above others while he did his work. This happened often during the school day. He does not remember it helping or making a difference. He never said anything regarding this because he deferred to the physical therapist. Thankfully, physical therapy services were received through an independent company beginning in junior high school and they continued through his junior year.

During lunch and recess, Clark found a way to be included. However, physical education was one class that was a very negative experience. At some point, his mother stated he was "never going to work with that man again." It was about sixth grade, and the physical education teacher told school staff and teachers to take away Clark's walker because he was becoming too dependent on it. Mother intervened, and Clark became an aide in the library, watering plants and reshelving books. He was happy but is not sure he did anything very useful. However, it was a better place to be than awkwardly trying to figure out what he was going to do while everybody else was participating in their physical education activity.

This experience was typical. For example, his physical education teacher might have planned basketball for the day and would not know how to accommodate "the student in the wheelchair." Although he was excluded because of the teacher's decision to not implement any accommodations, he feels he may have lucked out because he was not comfortable in the gymnasium to begin with and even now does not relish the thought of going to a gym.

Clark's favorite time of the day was his English class. He was always a reader. He liked reading and creative writing (which he studied in college). English was an area in which he excelled and he knew he was better than many others. In fact, Clark's bachelor's degree is in English. His master's degrees (yes, he has two) are in creative writing and public administration. He is currently in his third year as a doctoral student in public administration.

As mentioned previously, Clark hated both math and physical education. He did not attend any physical education classes while in high school. Clark's dad was a mechanical engineer and would attempt to help him with his math homework. After solving one problem, Clark was unable to solve another similar problem because it looked different; this was a source of great frustration to both his father and him. However, he had to take statistics in college, and he earned a B.

Clark remembers a time when he did not do his homework for several days, and his parents were eventually called by the principal and teachers. His parents asked why they had not been called much sooner, because they would have certainly intervened had they known of the situation. The faculty responded that his parents were going to have to recognize the fact that their son was never going to go to college. They believed his not doing his homework was indicative of the fact that he did not know what he was doing and his parents needed to come to terms with that; Clark's mother was not amused. Clark's feelings on the matter were that homework was unnecessary and beneath him; he simply did not care—a common deduction for a sixth grader.

To those teachers who conduct themselves in the above manner, Clark feels it would be great to remind everyone that, regardless of the years of experience one has as an educator or professional, remember that all students are different. "Do not rely on what you learned years ago or even last year; otherwise, you will not be able to meet students where they are—and if you do, you can be responsible for some serious damage or disservice because you are acting totally ignorant. Sometimes students need more than they are being given and sometimes they need less, but it is up to the teacher to pay attention to each individual student and ascertain what his or her needs are."

Regarding classmates, Clark jokes that he was neutral ground. He never got bullied due to his disability, but he often felt isolated. He had friends, but not close friends. It was not until later in life that he felt he learned *how* to make friends. Until that time, he thought his life was going to be lonely.

Clark "came out" the night before he departed for college. Therefore, his situation was convoluted—his disability helped cloak his sexual preference. If he hadn't had a disability, he believes life would have been harder because his peers would have recognized his preference in partners and would have been more judgmental.

When Clark told his parents about his preference in partners, they were concerned because they were very protective of him. They felt lucky to get him where he was and felt this was going to be just one more fight. "They were worried that they were not going to be able to protect me. They loved me and wanted me to be OK." After going away to college, he told a high school friend about his preference in partners, and the response was that his classmates thought he couldn't get a date and they didn't want to tease him.

For a person with a disability, coming out complicates life. People don't talk about this in school settings, but students have a lot of questions about sex. When one is young, sex is fascinating. Students wonder how the mechanics work and exactly what is going on with their bodies as they change.

How do people with disabilities express that part of themselves at a young age when they observe others going through the process of getting together and then breaking up? It's not typically thought that those with disabilities such as cerebral palsy are experiencing similar desires, so educators don't address the issue with them because they either don't want to or don't know how to address the topic. Clark understands that teachers have a lot on their plates academically. However, students with disabilities feel isolated and need to be included in all discussions.

Clark suggests that this conversation needs to occur with parents as well. It would help a young person learn how to develop friendships and ultimately how to navigate his or her world. These conversations should start early and address what the student thinks independence is going to look like, how the student is going to socialize with people, how the student is going to engage with people romantically, and how one is going to participate with others in a group setting or online. All these matters are discussed among one's peers, but when a person has a disability it's less likely that he or she will be included. So, it is most likely incumbent on the parents to educate their child regarding these matters.

It was always expected that Clark would go to college and live independently. Most conversations involving this part of his life occurred in high school. His parents were very involved in this discourse and helped research degree programs and schools that were accessible. Clark could not attend college in his home state because he would be unable to navigate in his wheelchair on the ice and snow. A university told him they could come out and deice his sidewalk for him, but he felt he was going to have a hard enough time attending school without imposing on someone to deice the sidewalk for him early on a cold winter morning.

Clark went on to college after high school because he wanted to prove he was not incapable in any way. He did not feel he was leaving many friends behind. Interestingly, Clark's high school counselors did not assist him by contacting different agencies that could help him transition to the postsecondary environment in regard to how he could access transportation, get funds to help with tuition or to get books paid for, receive tutoring at his receiving university, or access any campus services. He describes his counselors as nice people, but they were focused solely on the college application process. His high school was not in a small town, yet nobody gave him any information about what transitioning could look like (this is required by federal law to begin in ninth grade, but no later than eleventh grade). Fortunately, his university has a noted disabilities program that has been available to him. He has not needed to access it in the traditional sense, but occasionally he has used the computer lab.

When Clark was in high school, postsecondary goals included going to college. Clark had taken multiple English classes and received guidance from his counselor, and his parents supported his college goals. Originally, he intended to become a cartoonist or animator.

By the time he went to college, he dropped the idea of being a cartoonist and decided he was going to double major in painting and English. He quickly realized that his double major was going to cause him to be mediocre at both and good at neither. He describes painting as expensive, crazy, and time consuming. He muses about how he got through his classes as he never had enough time. He therefore dropped painting and focused on English.

After receiving his bachelor's degree, Clark's goal was to become an English professor, but he realized a bachelor's degree in English does not open that door; thus, he moved forward toward a master's degree in creative writing, not realizing how hard getting published was going to be. Because neither degree prepared him to teach, he obtained a job as an editor at a magazine. Eventually, he was offered a job in city government. He accepted the offer and became a city employee. He subsequently began taking doctorate-level public administration courses.

Clark has obtained all his degrees at one university and wonders whether or not that will make him less marketable. He sometimes thinks the only reason he has a job is that he is lucky. He fears at some point someone is going to be uncomfortable hiring him; this makes him anxious about the change that may be looming on the horizon as he is loyal and averse to change. He loves what he is currently doing.

The best and most enriching thing that has happened academically since high school is obtaining his degree in creative writing, as it was very personal. He wishes that earlier in life he recognized the gift he has to write creatively and generate some amazing poetry. The people who were most instrumental in inspiring him in this arena include various professors and peers. "Creative writing is interesting because people expect you to tell your story—that is, what your magic is made of—getting on paper that which is in your head."

His professors and peers appreciated his abilities although they occasionally disagreed on how to approach him when he wrote about his disability. Most creative writers think everything is a metaphor, but for Clark some things are definitely not, so it was a learning experience for everyone. In brief, his professors and peers got as much out of their experience together as he did: "It was a good relationship."

Upon reflection, Clark realizes that what his teachers did to help him be successful was to meet him on his own terms. It was clear that even though he is a self-proclaimed oddball, they allowed him to be creative with assignments in a way that was fun for him. School was not hard in an academic sense. The hardest part was figuring out how he was going to get through. Clark always gravitated toward adults because he felt they understood him better than his peers. They met him on his level and did not talk down to him.

Conversely, an example of a strategy that was done poorly was forcing him to take timed tests. Clark claims responsibility for this issue, however, as he had a desire to avoid accommodations that he could have taken advantage of that could have helped. He was therefore not allowing himself to benefit using the accommodations available to him and does not hold that against anyone. However, a good teacher would have recognized a pattern that twelve of the twenty questions were being answered on a consistent basis and therefore that was an acceptable number of questions to score for him or he needed more time to respond.

In public schools, Clark took standardized tests and typically completed the reading portion but not necessarily the math portion. He thinks taking standardized tests is a ritual. The value was that it prepared him for taking the SAT, which was necessary for college admissions. However, he believes that the teaching to the test that occurs in today's schools has no value. The things that interest Clark and many others are not on the tests.

Clark states that his parents never believed he was going to pursue a traditional path. What they wanted for him was to be happy in his endeavors, so they supported his wishes. His parents played a big, positive role throughout his life, saying they believed in him. When someone told him "no," they would tell them to "go stuff it!"

This does not mean parents should blindly believe their child is going to be a rocket scientist, but they do believe the path their child chooses to navigate their world is the appropriate one for them. "However one chooses to navigate, it is the way it should be done for that individual. If more people could understand that message, that would be a great improvement."

Clark posits that he got to this point in his life (a doctoral program) with a lot of luck and a lot of stubbornness. He does not think he has particularly good organizational skills. However, he is always willing to take on a challenge and describes himself as a bit crazy because he juggles too many things at one time. For example, he sometimes has to stay up all night to get his reading, writing, work, and volunteering done, so that is what he does. He believes his stubbornness has helped him succeed.

Clark believes he has always been capable of tackling new ideas. His current program (public administration) is very different from his former ones (English and creative writing), yet government is an enjoyable, novel area to study. He can see an entirely different way to employ his writing in regards to how government works. He thinks the way government works is miraculous.

"When one thinks about the human endeavor, it is touched, created, or ignored by government. Government is everything it chooses to do and everything that it chooses not to do, so it is everything. It can touch what one is interested in regarding art or in what artists do. It can be the way governments deal with people with disabilities. It can be the way government engages communities. It touches everything."

So, Clark feels he is lucky. He is in a position where he can make a positive difference. His goal as a government employee is to create solutions for the benefit of society by obtaining better outcomes.

Clark thinks the biggest misconception people have about those with cerebral palsy is that they are paralyzed and therefore have low mental capacity. "People often expect less of individuals with cerebral palsy than they expect of themselves due to this misinformed preconceived notion." This makes him wary. It's not entirely a joke when he says one of the reasons he is getting a doctorate degree is to show people that they are wrong. He is doing it because he is stubborn and he wants to put the last nail in that coffin.

Clark has advice to others who face challenges similar to his. Remember that "you have the ability to choose what to do with your life even if you have to have support with your daily living, even if you have to have support with making your way through life with a personal care attendant, or with a mobility device. Remember, it is just another tool in letting you be the one that charts your own course."

From his experience, he states, "You should not be afraid to admit you have a disability. Be comfortable in your own skin so you can succeed. If you have a disability with significant mental challenges, figure out how to share your life—when push comes to shove, it is not just how you relate to each other, but how you relate to the rest of the world. Don't let anyone put you in a box. Find resources that let you help yourself."

On behalf of his mother, Clark would like to say that all that has happened to him might not have happened if, when she went into the hospital thinking she was in labor, the doctor had not told her she was having prelabor pains and sent her home. When she returned to the hospital a few hours later, it was the nurse who emphatically expressed to the doctor that there was an issue. Mother was indeed embarking on a difficult labor and a difficult C-section ensued. Clark believes it was the arrogance of this doctor who indiscriminately dismissed his mother when she needed medical attention that resulted in his being bound to walkers and wheelchairs for life. "Doctors and educators need to be open-minded, remember there are multiple possibilities, approaches, and outcomes, and be willing to admit they are not all knowing. They can be so very wrong and not take appropriate action until it is too late."

Read this story and be humbled. Arrogance is not worth another person's life. Things may have worked out the same, but Clark doubts it.

TIPS FOR TEACHERS OF ORTHOPEDICALLY IMPAIRED STUDENTS

- Provide preferential seating.
- Offer flexible time limits to navigate and get situated.
- Question the student regarding his or her speed issues, for example, verbal response time to questions, writing or keyboard speed, and navigation ability in case of emergency.
- Discuss medical conditions and whether the student is easily fatigued or develops sores or pain when in one position for period of time.
- Provide frequent breaks or changes in position as necessary.
- If the impairment affects fine-motor control, reduce assignment questions.
- Offer special grips for pens and pencils if the impairment affects writing.
- Permit oral response if writing is too difficult.
- Consider the use of a note taker.
- Provide copies of presentations.

- If appropriate, reduce or eliminate the need to copy from the board.
- Provide a larger desk, lap tray, or table as necessary.
- Present material on the student's dominant side unless otherwise instructed by a therapist.
- Create a restroom break signal between you and the student.
- Discuss with the therapist how to maximize time on task.
- Evaluate for assistive technology needs.
- Arrange the room for wheelchair or walker mobility.
- Ensure that every activity is accessible to the student.
- Teach classmates to assist only when asked by the student with the impairment.
- Build on the student's strengths.
- Ensure that the student can always see you and the visual displays to which you are referring.

TIPS FOR PARENTS OF ORTHOPEDICALLY IMPAIRED STUDENTS

- Seek the assistance and advice of other parents.
- Recognize that you are not alone.
- Do not become overwhelmed; recognize that mistakes will be made.
- Take one day at a time.
- Learn special education terminology.
- Seek information from various resources.
- Keep daily routines as normal as possible.
- Maintain a positive outlook.
- Take care of yourself.
- Search for optional program alternatives.
- Teach your child to self-advocate.
- Help your child learn to problem solve—this is empowering.
- Encourage independence—let your child help with chores, teach him or her to budget, help him or her learn to manage any necessary medication.
- Help your child learn to set goals that are achievable.

TIPS FOR STUDENTS WITH AN ORTHOPEDIC IMPAIRMENT

- Self-advocate—Communicate your personal learning style and mobility needs to your teachers.
- Inform your teachers of the accommodations listed in your IEP.
- Seek peer support from your classmates.

- Learn about peer support groups both in and out of school.
- Look for study groups that are respectful of your needs.
- If you cannot access a standard computer workstation, request an adjustable-height table or adaptable keyboard.
- If you are in college, connect with your disability service office to learn about available services and supports.
- Familiarize yourself with ACCESS *Self-Advocacy Handbook for College Students with Disabilities.*
- Ask if your college has priority registration.
- If class attendance or mobilization is difficult, consider alternative formats such as computer-based instruction or online learning.
- Plan ahead for accessible transportation, particularly when considering the postsecondary environment.
- If books in an alternative format are needed, inform your disability service office in a timely manner so they can be ordered or current books can be converted.
- Ask if the lecture can be recorded if needed or if you can have a note taker.
- Request an ergonomic evaluation as needed.
- Develop a plan of action for both short- and long-term goals.
- Be aware of your strengths as well as your challenges—you need to know yourself and how to get what you need.

REFERENCES

Access Project, Department of Occupational Therapy, Colorado State University. (2010). *Learning strategies: What can the student do?* Retrieved from http://accessproject.colostate.edu/ disability/modules/MI/tut_MI.cfm?display=pg_8.

Heart of Illinois Low Incidence Association, Tri-County Special Education Association. (2008). *Helping students with orthopedic, hearing, or visual impairments succeed in the classroom.* Retrieved from http://www.tcsea.org/downlaods/helping_ students.pdf.

Kuehnel, A. (n.d.). *Special education characteristics, accommodations, and strategies.* Retrieved from http://akuehnel3.tripod.com/id7.html.

Paul, J., & Epanchin, B. (1991). *Educating emotionally disturbed children and youth: Theories and practices for teachers* (2nd ed.). New York: Macmillan.

Chapter 4

Craig's Parents' Story

Autism Spectrum Disorder

Craig is the middle child of six siblings in a loving family. He was a happy child in spite of needing a set of tubes in his ears his first year of life and fighting an unknown condition thought to be blood poisoning six months later. While fighting blood poisoning, Craig's organs began shutting down. His mother rushed him to his pediatrician, who had him immediately admitted to the hospital. For twenty-four heart-wrenching hours, multiple tests were run in an attempt to determine what was going on with Craig's little body. His parents felt frantic and helpless.

In a desperate stopgap measure to save him, antibiotics were administered. After a long, exhausting night of crying, fretting, and waiting, and for some reason unknown even to his doctors, Craig's organs slowly began functioning again. He gradually recovered and was eventually able to stand in his crib. The doctors never did discover a medical reason for this inexplicable onset of symptoms or Craig's sudden recovery.

After the harrowing events of the night had come to a joyful conclusion, Mom and Dad were told that Craig almost did not make it. This is the only time in Craig's eighteen years of life that his organs shut down. His parents felt that they had successfully faced the ultimate fear of all parents: losing their child.

A subsequent anxious moment occurred when Craig experienced some seizure activity. He was temporarily medicated, but that decision was reversed because it made him lethargic. His pediatrician decided it was better to monitor him; he progressed and grew, never experiencing seizures again.

The doctor's decision to take Craig off medication pleased his parents because "the medications changed the essence of Craig, and we never wanted to do that."

When Craig was two and a half years old, his parents noted something was markedly wrong due to an apparent speech and language delay. They took him to their family doctor, who referred them to a psychologist for diagnosis. Father remembers Craig having fun during his testing "because they made it like a game for him."

After testing, Craig was sitting between both parents as they were given the diagnosis of "autism," which was disclosed in a very cold, direct, matter-of-fact manner. The parents looked at each other wondering why they were receiving such grave news and where the hope could be found in such a word. They yearned for information that would help them. Father remembers both of their mouths hanging open in disbelief. They couldn't believe this was happening to their little Craig because "he was such a happy, good kid."

Autism is a neural development disorder that is usually exhibited as impaired social communication, limited language skills, poor eye contact, and repetitive motion. These signs occur prior to the age of three years. The severity of this disorder lies on a broad spectrum known as the autism spectrum disorder (ASD), with some individuals presenting fewer symptoms to a smaller degree than others.

The most severe form of ASD is autism, a milder form is Asperger's syndrome, and finally there is childhood disintegrative disorder and pervasive developmental disorder not otherwise specified (PDD-NOS). Usually, individuals with a diagnosis of ASD are preoccupied with certain items or subjects and thrive when their day is very structured and routine. The intensity of these symptoms varies from individual to individual. Often, with exceptions, ASD individuals are not able to live independently when they reach adulthood.

For Craig's young parents, "receiving the diagnosis of autism felt like a grim breaking point. It was like running into a giant brick wall," made more difficult by the cold manner in which the condition was described. Craig's parents were told he would have this condition throughout his life. Statements such as, "He will never be able to get around on his own," "He will never be affectionate," and "He will never be able to travel" felt earth shattering.

The list of obstacles was long and both parents wondered, "How in the world are we going to make it? We felt blindsided, not knowing where this was coming from; it felt so overwhelming." As tenacious parents who normally tell their children they are capable of doing anything, their reaction was not to step back and say, "You're right." Rather, their reaction was to question, "How can you say this about my child?"

Both parents were in tears, yet the psychologist remained cold and just very matter-of-fact. At the end the psychologist said, "I hope I'm wrong," and Mother retorted, "I know you're wrong." When walking out of that meeting, they felt as if they had just been run over by a Mack truck. Throughout all their subsequent adversities, there was never a time when they did not believe they were going to make it. They both remark, "It has been Craig who has provided us with inspiration all along the way." Yet the anger felt when Craig's distressing diagnosis befell them in such a cold manner has not been forgotten.

After leaving the psychologist's office, the parents returned to the pediatrician's office to talk to her about the crushing news they had just received. "The pediatrician was in shock and said she couldn't believe what she was hearing. She did a great job resetting the foundation by explaining that there was no way Craig could be a 9 on a scale from 1 to 10 (with 10 being the worst) because developmentally he would not be walking, jumping, and functioning as well as he does." She gave the parents permission to "throw the ominous diagnosis out the window."

Additionally, at the end of her workday, this doctor devoted six hours of her time to Craig's parents and stated they would work together as a team to raise him. She directed Mother to never, ever stop fighting for Craig, emphasizing that no one was going to do anything for her and she was going to have to fight for everything in Craig's behalf. They continue to gratefully embrace the perceptive advice from their incredible, young doctor.

That evening, after they returned home from their exhausting ordeal, they were lying on the bed trying to digest all the information they had received. Craig toddled in and said, "Mama" and "Dada." They looked at each other and knew that there was hope.

Mother and Father were told by their doctor to visit the organization Raising Special Kids. They were not told what the organization did (it provides parent-to-parent support, information, individual assistance, and training at no cost) or why they were being referred there. They had never heard of this group and were distraught thinking that they would need such intensive assistance. "Our reality had changed; everything was so surreal." Although their minds were racing, they wanted to ensure that they were not in denial and were being realistic regarding Craig's current and future needs. New to the diagnosis, they felt unsure how to define what they were hearing so they could accurately decipher what to do with the information.

At the time Craig was diagnosed, there were four children in the family and Craig's mother was in college working on her master's degree in psychology. Thus, she and her husband were aware that Craig struggled, but they were unaware it could be to the extent of possibly facing very limited life experiences. Initially, they were sure the diagnosis was incorrect. As time passed, they came to terms with what they faced and made a decision that their family was going to be about equity and inclusion for everyone, no exceptions. They decided to move forward with their plans to have a large family and not allow this one diagnosis to set the tone for what life would be like for Craig or for the family. Every child would participate in vacations, birthday parties, and traveling.

Attaining this goal has required consistency that guides the family through the maze of difficulties they have faced—including being judged by others, even relatives who encouraged them to place Craig in day care. However, Mother and Father created their own plan as a couple, which included sacrificing material comforts while they kept Craig at home in order to nurture him and provide for his needs. "We were going to let Craig become the person he was meant to become." Father credits Mother with Craig's progress and says, "She is the center of our world. If it were not for her obtaining her knowledge and being the person she is, Craig very likely would have fallen through the cracks."

Mother and Father chose to not make demands as parents. They customized their parenting to who their children were because they wanted them to feel free to express themselves and be creative without the parents' placing restrictions on this process. They had discussions with their children during which they emphasized the importance of family, how they were going to respect one another, and emphasized that they were going to exist well. They encouraged solidifying the family as a unit as they faced a very difficult world.

Craig's mother took him to an early intervention program at the local university approximately one month after receiving his diagnosis. He was evaluated and accepted into the program, which he attended with Mother three days a week for about an hour and a half each day until he was four years old. The staff members worked with him one-on-one, provided speech and language services, and taught him to sign. The environment was very busy and involved play therapy and outdoor play. Craig occasionally interacted with other children but usually enjoyed singular play.

At age four, Craig was transitioned to the Head Start program. Head Start provides educational, nutritional, health, and social services to preschool children. He attended three days a week for three hours each morning. Unlike his previous program, Head Start consisted of more structure then play; this structure was ultimately more detrimental for Craig because he needed more flexibility.

One of the biggest issues that became a resounding theme as Craig moved through the education system began in the Head Start environment. Craig, who had a very slight build, would not eat certain foods with textures he could not stomach. Staff members, who did not know about common autistic issues such as this, disapproved of his food choices. Additionally, much to the staff's dismay, Craig was prone to roam about the room while eating his food; thus, lunch time was a daily struggle.

Staff had multiple side conversations, implying Mother was enabling him and depriving him of appropriate nutrition. Mother repeatedly explained Craig's diagnosis and texture issues, but her message fell on deaf ears. She asserted that there are certain foods adults do not want to eat; likewise, Craig did not want to eat certain foods. She also noted that Craig's pediatrician knew about his food choices and they had collaboratively created a plan to ensure that his nutritional needs were met. However, this remained an issue and created immense stress for Craig, so Mother removed him from Head Start. "I understood they did not know about autism but found it frustrating that they were not open to learning about it."

Father gives his wife credit for advocating for Craig in the face of criticism from both his school and various relatives, who also implied that Craig was not eating sensibly. They indicated he should be force-fed. Craig's parents would not buckle to their demands and made it clear that he was not abused or neglected, just being allowed to make choices regarding his life. "The difference was rather than forcing him to do what I wanted; I was giving him tools to learn how to live life. I was not going to sit there and insist that Craig live my way because that would result in internal turmoil and failure as a parent."

This issue reared its ugly head again when Craig was in kindergarten. Mother was asked to attend a conference. When she arrived, the school psychologist, nurse, and others were in attendance. "The purpose of the meeting was to lecture me on how to feed my son nutritious meals." Again, his thin build was referred to as evidence of her neglect.

Mother tearfully defended herself and explained that children on the autism spectrum have texture issues with certain foods. She retorted, "You can call Craig's pediatrician to acquire information regarding his health status because tests have been run and his nutrition is in balance." During this meeting, mother was advised to put Craig on medication so that he could focus during class. Although she was opposed, mother agreed to discuss the issue with Craig's pediatrician. Craig was briefly prescribed Adderall but was taken off it after two months because it made him extremely sleepy. Father describes times at home when Craig would fall asleep in the living room in the middle of the day with commotion all around him.

The day after this meeting occurred, Mother received a note from Craig's kindergarten teacher, who had attended the meeting. She had written a five-page letter describing what an incredible person Craig's mother was and how horrible she felt about the things that were said. She also explained that she would allow him to sleep during class as needed because his lethargy was clearly a result of his medication. This letter was liberating because it affirmed that Craig was going to get what he needed and this teacher understood those needs. "This kindergarten teacher was sensitive to Craig and seemed to intuitively know what he needed. For example, Craig liked snakes, so this teacher would bring a stuffed snake to class and wrap it around her neck for Craig to enjoy; she clearly connected with him." Mother and Father have remained forever grateful to this teacher for reaching out to them.

One of the looming concerns that resulted from these negative exchanges was whether or not the system was going to take Craig away from the family. Mother worried that the school was going to file neglect charges against her. She felt badgered and crushed.

"I felt like I had to defend my choices and actions over and over again. I wished people understood I was not trying to be difficult and wanted them just to take my word for it. I was not trying to make anything harder for anyone; rather, I was trying to inform others regarding the needs of my child. I wanted them to listen to me, not judge me or insist that I conform to their program."

Halfway through third grade, Craig's teacher requested a meeting with Mother and stated she did not feel she could have Craig in her class anymore because "all he wants to do is read while he is in here," and that it was disruptive to her as a teacher. Mother said, "Clearly this classroom is not the place for him because we encourage reading as an important aspect of his growth. Since you don't approve of this, I will see to it that he is placed in a class where reading is encouraged." Mother wanted to say, "Are you hearing yourself? When Craig was first diagnosed we were told he would never be able to read. We are thrilled to hear such news!"

Both parents found this discussion shocking because they had requested this teacher for their son. They knew her and believed she had his best interests at heart. Furthermore, they were confused because Craig had an individualized education program (IEP), went to resource classes, and was in inclusion to the greatest extent possible. "It's not like she didn't know Craig had a disability. This was another heartache and great disappointment especially for Craig, something we feel he didn't deserve."

They describe this as "blatant discrimination—he should not have had to have been removed from that class." Both parents struggled with the decision they made to switch classes because it meant their son had to leave his friends. On the other hand, they felt they could not leave him in a class where the teacher did not approve of his reading.

Mother left the meeting, went directly to the principal, and stated that Craig needed to be placed in another classroom. It was extremely devastating telling Craig that he would be in a new room with a new teacher and have to make new friends, as this was disruptive to his routine. When asked why he couldn't be with his same friends, Mother attempted to smooth the impending transition by describing the opportunity he was going to have to make new friends. She felt as if she once again had to clean up another educator's mess.

Father asserts there were multiple times throughout Craig's education when his rights were violated and his parents could have filed suit against his school. However, they believed the repercussions against them, their family, their other children, and mostly Craig, would have been detrimental and ultimately would not obtain the results they were seeking. They wanted Craig to be treated like every other child with equal opportunities to learn within the parameters of his diagnosis. In the long run the question with which they wrestled was whether they were hurting or helping their son. They describe moments like these as "a tough judgment call that had to be made many times over the years."

Craig's parents feel he was not harassed by his peers in elementary school as that age group is so forgiving and inoculated to the biases they regretfully tend to learn later in life. This changed around the period of junior high school. When bullied, Craig would not tattle on his peers. Instead, his parents would learn about the indiscretions and bullying when his siblings would hear others talk about it.

Sometimes this information would be discovered many years after the incident. In high school, there was a time when Craig was being bullied and he told his mother he was not sure he belonged in this world, and maybe the bullying was entirely his fault. Mother affirmed he had a place in this world and his family all felt the same way. (Craig is currently a high school graduate yet Father states he just learned some information about his being bullied when he was in the eighth grade.)

Clearly, investigating situations was difficult to carry out in a timely manner due to Craig's unwillingness to "rat out" his friends (described by Father as a blessing and a curse). Fortunately, his siblings and their friends were always very protective of him. However, this presented another problem as these protectors could get themselves in trouble when they stood up for Craig in an effort to protect him.

Craig's parents pleaded with each school to believe them if they said there was a bullying problem. They made it clear that Craig's siblings were not to be punished if they stepped in to protect their brother. Navigating through these bullying issues was extremely difficult and a constant challenge. The overarching issue was how any student could learn when he was in constant fear for his safety. Craig's parents believe battling bullying and creating safe schools can be accomplished by providing programs that train both students and teachers. They offered to fund a social and diversity training program at Craig's high school via a consultant who works with Oprah Winfrey, but the school never accepted this gracious offer.

Craig told Dad he couldn't hate anyone, even those who hurt him. The only time Dad has ever heard any of his children express anger against anyone is when these other people hurt Craig. Craig states he does not know why people want to mistreat him. He internalizes these issues and wonders if it is he, and whether it is because he is not a good person. Understanding this issue is confusing for him and makes him wonder if he needs to change his behavior or if he has done something wrong that caused the other person to lash out against him.

His parents state, "Explaining others' rude behavior is tough." Craig will sometimes cheerfully ask his mother if he can be mean. She will say no, that we don't treat others that way. They will joke and say he can be mean to his brother when he returns home from college—Craig understands this implies bantering in a playful way. So, Mother tries to have this conversation in a lighthearted manner in a way that Craig understands that when people are mean, it is not about him.

Regarding people who supported Craig, his parents recall an elementary teacher's aide who was extraordinary. She was about twenty-two years old and had a very nurturing, caring personality. She would constantly give Mother confidence and support and let her know that she was going to take care of Craig.

This aide honored Craig's learning style and food requirements. But it was the genuineness with which she conducted herself that really made an impression. She worked with Craig for about two years. Afterward, he did not have an aide. Instead, he was placed into a resource class.

Another supportive person was a library aide. In fact, the parents recall mainly that it was the support staff in Craig's early years who provided for him and assisted with his needs as opposed to the certified staff who were supposed to be "educated." Currently, classroom aides' presence in schools is very limited due to the economic downturn. However, they seem to be the ones who always excelled by providing extra time, care, and support.

Mother notes that Craig has not cried since he was about four years old, although he will have an occasional expression of sadness. She speculates this is because he sees the world differently, and this prevents him from suffering and grieving in the same way as others. When other family members have passed away and the family has been grieving, Craig puts on a big smile and states they are "going to the big concert in the sky. They are going to be OK." Given Craig's character and his love for music, this explanation clearly shows how he views the world.

Mother states that she has learned much more from Craig than what she believes she has given to him. When Mother wants to be angry or hateful, she tells herself she has no right. She thinks of Craig and how he does not hate. "It keeps me balanced; it keeps my life in perspective and causes me to step back. I feel so thankful and grateful to Craig because he has allowed me to see the world differently. I can look beyond my initial expectations of other people because of what I have learned from Craig. I have learned that some individuals are not capable of meeting my expectations because they operate in a different way and that's OK—probably better."

Regarding the IEP process, Craig's parents believe it was appropriately implemented. Academics were not an issue; rather, Craig's social needs were. To this day, they want Craig to be treated as a person first because the academic piece will follow.

Craig is a very active learner who has the desire to please and wants to do everything that is asked of him. Mother has never had to prod him to complete any work. He has been self-regulating as much as he can be given his exceptionality. Furthermore, Mother believes her voice was heard and her concerns were addressed during the IEP meetings. However, especially early on, she believes it would have been beneficial if she could have informed Craig's teachers about autism and the school could have informed her about the special education process.

"As a young mother I was learning and didn't know what to ask because I did not have any experience in this arena, did not know anybody with a special needs child, and had no relatives with a special needs child in whom I could confide. This is true of so many parents. You have to trust what school personnel are telling you because they are the professionals. Parents don't want to look like an idiot. They believe school personnel are the experts who will do the best they can to provide for each child. Parents therefore trust that the plan being created is a good one, believing in the compassion and education of the provider."

Father and Mother state, "Signing an IEP is akin to signing mortgage papers. Pages are initialed or signed without a clear understanding of exactly what is on the written page. It seems appropriate and so you just go with it."

In elementary and junior high school, Craig received speech-language services as well as occupational therapy, and made appropriate progress toward his goals. His parents never felt as if there were any lapses with the ancillary staff. Craig was a rule follower and did what was expected of him; he was very disciplined and focused. The only disappointments they recall were with the general education teachers in his earlier years. "The ones who were supposed to be the most educated were the ones who were the biggest disappointments. It wasn't that they weren't educated; it was their unwillingness to learn about autism. They just weren't interested."

Throughout his schooling, there was an ongoing debate regarding whether Craig had Asperger's syndrome or autism. "This was the question of the day. At that time, nobody really knew. One school psychologist reasoned he had Asperger's stating, 'I dated a guy who had Asperger's and Craig is just like that, so Craig is going to be just fine. Don't worry, he is a good-looking kid and people in this world accept and treat good-looking people better than bad-looking people.'" His parents could not believe what they heard and just looked at each other in disbelief, wondering, "Did I really just hear that?"

Mother's advice to parents who are new to navigating the education system is to take a trusted friend or relative to their child's IEP meeting—not necessarily a spouse. "Our stress may cause us to forget certain items that need to be addressed. A good friend gives us comfort and helps us network. Pending IEP meetings can cause great anxiety because parents often feel very overwhelmed having to defend their child's issues and advocate for them. Creating an environment that is not intense is helpful. Remember, this is all about the child."

Father adds, "Scholastic achievement does not imply expertise. People tell parents things they learned from a book that may be meaningless for their child." He agrees having a third party present is important. "As parents new to the process, no one can tell you what is better for your child than you. When your heart is in the right place you can't go wrong."

Father recalls that during Craig's last IEP meeting in high school, the discussion regarding Craig's transitioning to college occurred. Every time this was mentioned the adults would grow very somber and comment that they were going to greatly miss him. Father responded he was lucky because he was going to get to keep him.

Craig's parents believe his high school teachers were wonderful. "This is where most of Craig's positive experiences occurred. Teachers made an effort to get to know him, considered this to be a privilege, and appreciated him as a person. His team of special education teachers was composed of some awesome characters. They were trustworthy and caring."

Mother and Father also commend Craig's speech-language pathologist, who worked with him in a group setting so he could improve his social interactions. Mother believes, however, that it was his brother who helped solidify his peer relationships. Outside school, sleepovers and other similar peer interactions helped Craig learn how to navigate social environments. Craig wanted to be a part of the conversations, so he learned how from his older peers. Mother also senses that having his brother and his brother's friends on campus ultimately gave him the companionship he needed, which in turn allowed Craig to experience high school the way he should.

Mother believes that in high school, Craig had the appropriate amount of support as well as appropriate classes. However, placing him in electives was a challenge. "Craig would ask to try various classes, sometimes some that were not appropriate such as foreign language. It was difficult to find appropriate matches. Physical education was even a difficult placement because it was so large, so loud, and so chaotic."

To navigate this requirement, Craig was placed in an adaptive PE class as the designated assistant. Craig questioned why he was in there because he knew he was physically more capable than that population. Mother explained he was their helper and this pleased Craig, contributing to a successful experience. Issues such as these caused Craig's parents to occasionally wonder if homeschooling him would be a better choice. They ultimately decided against it because they did not want him to miss the opportunity to have social interactions, specifically, in his elective classes, which he enjoyed immensely. Also, Craig was a rule follower and understood that going to school is what you do every day.

Craig's parents remark there is no one better time of day than another; his temperament is pretty even throughout the day. They never had to struggle to send him to school. He was always up and dressed, with his backpack and a smile on, ready to go. His parents are grateful he's able to stay on an even keel in spite of the difficult experiences he occasionally faces. Adults have commented that they wish they were half as happy as Craig. Father admires Craig's ability to maintain self-control when harassed, stating, "It brings me to my knees. Craig's joy overwhelms people. Once you know him, he owns your heart."

Regarding the No Child Left Behind Act and its testing requirement, Craig's parents state that they do not believe standardized testing is appropriate for anybody. Mother knew that per his IEP he was not going to be held to the standard. As for Craig, he knew everybody else was taking this test and was looking forward to being included.

Mother states it would have been more challenging for her to have to tell him to not go with his friends and test. That would have sent the message that he was different from his friends. So, from that end, it was a routine matter—testing was something everybody was doing. Making the environment fit his world and what he was expecting was positive. Father notes that Craig's scores improved every year that he took the test: "He always gave his best effort."

Father's fondest memory is when Craig graduated. The ceremony was greeted with a collective sigh of relief from the whole family. They felt all the hoops had been jumped through, all the sacrifices had been made, and all the criteria had been met. It was a very emotional event for everyone.

A family friend returned home specifically for this event. When Craig saw him, he broke into a run and threw his arms around this friend. It was perfect to see him so elated. During the ceremony, Craig's principal recognized him as being exceptional by achieving significant feats that are usually not measured, celebrated, or touted sufficiently.

Nothing the doctors initially predicted ultimately came to fruition. For example, Craig knows how to ride a bike, play guitar, respond to people, work on computers, and roughhouse with his siblings. He is very affectionate. Furthermore, he just completed his first year of community college. Father states that they talked to Craig about being a college student his whole life and painted it as a positive experience. However, no person or organization assisted the family as they attempted to transition Craig from high school to the postsecondary environment. Mother speculates this might be because they had stated Craig was going to attend community college.

Overall, both parents have been extremely disappointed in the college experience. They did not know that at the college level, modifications to the curriculum did not exist, only accommodations. This means that a student with a disability is expected to complete the entire required syllabus just like his general education peers. Accommodations such as extra time to complete work are permitted, but the amount of work is the same for everyone.

To help Craig enroll in community college, Mother provided his IEP to the disability service office to ensure that the college was informed of his diagnosis and needs. She made a follow-up appointment with the director of the disability service office and found her to be very fragmented, providing no guidance and appearing to not know how to support the needs of an autistic student. When asked about evening courses, which would place Craig with more mature people, Mother was told Craig needed to be assessed. The director took him back for his assessments and then informed Mother thirty minutes later that she did not believe there was a place for Craig because he had not begun his test. "He has only completed his name and does not know his zip code. If this is where he is I don't think this is going to work." Mother asked how the director was assessing him and she said, "With pencil and paper." Mother reminded her that his IEP said he needed to do everything on the computer and she thought the director had read this.

Mother felt devastated to think this was going to be the level of support Craig was going to receive in this environment. After all, if this was what was occurring during his initial assessment, this was a bad sign. Craig was so excited to be at college that Mother was determined he was going to have a good first experience. Mother insisted they put him on the computer. Within forty-five minutes, he completed his math and reading assessment. She wanted to say, "I told you so but you were ready to send me out the door." She firmly believes had she not been there as an advocate, the encounter would have resulted in disaster.

Craig was excited to attend college. He asked Father to shave him so he would look clean-cut when he attended classes. (To enroll him, mother ensured that the Family Educational Rights and Privacy Act [FERPA] was in place.) Although he was very happy to be a college student, he had not expressed a desire to major in anything particular. He likes music, bicycling, and pets. He comments that he would like to open a bike shop, but he is very sensitive to pets' needs, so his parents speculate that grooming might be an appropriate career to explore.

A retired teacher friend decided to take a guitar class at the community college and offered to take Craig with him. Mother e-mailed the instructor and let her know that FERPA was in place. As the semester progressed, the teacher contacted Mother and praised Craig for his eager participation. She went above and beyond the call of duty by informing mother she was going to miss the class due to illness and she didn't want Craig to show up and be lost or disappointed when no one was there. That experience worked out incredibly.

Also, one of Mother's colleagues got hired as an adjunct faculty member at the community college. This colleague has a son with autism and was therefore empathetic to the needs of this population. Craig's parents enrolled him in this colleague's class. Craig had a wonderful experience and received As in both classes. However, there were a couple of assignments that were a little more in depth, requiring a bibliography as well as research; this increased his level of stress. This experience reminded Mother that she needs to continually seek knowledge in order to appropriately advocate for her son, that his education needs to occur in baby steps. Her plan is to ask Craig if he wants to take classes, not insist that he take them. She would like to remind society as a whole that this population of autistic people is growing in number and it would benefit all of us to learn about autism in order to better provide for their needs.

Because learning material in a college textbook is challenging for an autistic student, Mother feels at a loss as to how she is going to ensure that Craig receives further education. She feels very disheartened. She believes that with the right tools and assistance, he is capable of learning anything. He does have his own laptop and is permitted to have a note taker. Mother states that it would be helpful if someone texted his daily work to her and if he could have a tutor while he is at school. Craig has difficulty understanding the logistics of when work is due. Because she is not in the class, Mother does not know when assignments are due either, but she cannot quit her job to attend class with him. "This has become just one more thing to manage."

Mother understands Craig can handle only about two classes at a time but feels that is OK as she has no time limit for him to graduate. She does not want Craig to feel anxious about these issues. "Craig is a young man who wants to make his mark on the world like any other young man. All I'm asking for is a good environment that is age appropriate for him."

Mother feels she always has to plan for Craig, and this is exhausting work. However, she does not want him to regress by being left home all day while she and Father are at work. Craig has commented that he is not bored when he is at home alone. To the contrary, he enjoys the quiet, being able to sleep in, and enjoying the computer for as long as he wants. Mother recognizes this may actually be a good time for him in spite of her concerns about making his world right. She knows her role has changed but does not know what it should look like at this point.

There is no plan for the current semester because both parents feel apprehensive. However, they are considering a cycling class and an online computer class. (Craig asks when he is going to start every day.) They are not worried about Craig; rather, they are worried about the others around him and their impact on him. Mother says, "My son has been knocked down, made fun of, degraded, and humiliated during his eighteen years of life, and I will not allow it to happen and just stand by as long as I live." She admits that Craig does not get as demoralized by other people's actions as she does.

Craig's parents have discussed a second career as record store owners since Craig has a broad knowledge of many musical facts that he would enjoy sharing, such as the instruments musicians play and how many they own. He downloads various genres of music and is familiar with all of them. Pursuing a dream like this would be ideal because Craig would not just exist, he would be living. Mother wants him to have the best life imaginable, traveling with him and exposing him to multiple experiences. Craig could continue to be educated through his parents as they provide an array of experiences for him. Mother is determined to show him as much of the world as she can to broaden his horizons through learning, building, and creating. As this is occurring, Mother acknowledges she will also be learning—probably more than Craig. Father states he learned much in college but even more from his peers, and believes this can be true for Craig as well.

Craig would like a job, his independence, and the ability to live on his own. He doesn't want to drive. He desires independence just like that of his older brother. Trying to fit that into place for him at some point in the future is something his parents would like to do. He might transition to independence by living with one of his siblings, or his parents might move to another state with mild weather and a good mass transit system.

Craig likes to be outdoors, but safety is a concern as he is not fully aware of issues such as watching for people backing out of their driveways. He also still needs reminders about the rules of the road, such as coming to a full stop at a stop sign. He does currently cycle on the same neighborhood path every day, and this helps keep him safe.

Mother believes if they had accepted the initial diagnosis, it would have definitely limited Craig's success. "Just because somebody has pronounced a grim diagnosis, it doesn't necessarily make it so. At the time of Craig's diagnosis of autism, information was new and evolving. The process of having to address Craig's daily needs has never been easy, as it has required constant learning through trial and error, learning what will work, and if that doesn't work what is the next way to approach the issue. When one has a child with autism, it is not the child that needs to be navigated but the world around them. Therein lies the dilemma. You are trying to decide how to navigate and inform the community that this is who my son is, this is who I am, and if we make that okay for him things will be fine."

Craig has walked away with many great lessons from his parents that have contributed to his being the healthy, happy, incredible man he is today. He has unconditional love, reliable advice, modeling of being responsible, and love of life. His parents have advocated for him so he can experience opportunities he would not have had otherwise. Father aptly sums it up by saying, "Life is about moments that take your breath away, and Craig is a constant reminder of that."

TIPS FOR TEACHERS OF AUTISM SPECTRUM DISORDERED STUDENTS

Sequence tasks.
Use concrete language.
Practice turn taking.
Provide fewer choices.
Reword instructions if they appear misunderstood.
Break tasks into small steps.
Avoid idioms, for example, "Put on your thinking caps."
Use visual representations such as photos, objects, or line drawings to illustrate what you want.
Consider various modes of the aforementioned visual support: static (print or object based), dynamic (movement and sound), interactive (requires student involvement).
Choose the same clue words that mean the routine will change.
Teach to all modalities.
Minimize distractions and overstimulation.
Link work to student's interest.
Use technology as appropriate.
Guard against bullying.
Find alternatives to activities, for example, the teacher's helper during PE.
Use sign language if appropriate.
Place in an inclusive environment.
Provide peer tutoring.
Provide video modeling to illustrate social communication, nonverbal communication play, daily living skills, making requests, community outings, responding to requests, or responding to teasing.

Seat away from noisy fluorescent lights or humming fans.

Role-play.

Communicate regularly with parents via e-mail or phone (don't rely on notes' getting delivered).

TIPS FOR PARENTS OF AUTISM SPECTRUM DISORDERED CHILDREN

Tips to Help Your Elementary School–Aged Child

Read recipes and stories.

Measure ingredients.

Compare foods.

Sort items.

Write shopping lists.

Go to the public library during story time.

Participate in crafts at the community center.

Visit museums.

Take photos of your neighborhood.

Use pictures to show what you want.

Create a list of new words.

Make a puppet to represent a story character.

Spell words on a shopping list.

Estimate costs of items.

Label objects.

Organize shelves.

Write letters to people you know.

Tips to Help Your High School–Aged Child

Make bedtime the same time every night.

Teach alternative responses, for example, "That is one way to approach the situation, what's another?"

Establish code words or motions for needs such as time out from a situation.

Provide alternatives, for example, "You cannot hit your brother, but you can go to your room and play on your computer until you are not upset."

Keep favorite foods available.

Motivate by stating the reward waiting when a task is completed, for example, "You may watch one hour of television when you are done with your book report."

Implement modest goals that are attainable.

Rehearse to prepare your child for an impending difficult situation.

List rules or routines on a calendar.

Never withhold necessities as a consequence, for example, food, medicine, water.

Schedule downtime for decompression and soothing activities.

Reward positive behavior.

Seek volunteer options within the community.

Encourage thinking time so your teen can think of alternative, positive solutions.

Honor special interests.

Redirect if your child has a short attention span.

Teach self-care skills.

Preteach appropriate behaviors.

Establish a physical cue to calm your anxious child, for example, a hand on the shoulder or a wink.

Give verbal praise for appropriate behavior.

Share one message at a time.

Allow natural consequences to occur.

Keep in mind that ignoring behavior sometimes extinguishes it.

Engage in active listening, for example, look at your child and respond with appropriate voice tone.

Be cognizant that inappropriate behavior is not necessarily misbehavior.

Tips to Help Your College-Aged Child

Transition slowly; consider starting at a community college.

Consider living at home before attempting to live in a dorm or apartment.

Take only a few classes each semester.

Educate yourself regarding the differences between Individuals with Disabilities Education Act (IDEA) and the Americans with Disabilities Act (ADA).

Ensure that the disability service office and your child's professors are aware of the diagnosis.

Be prepared to seek additional support to cope with anxiety, stress, or fear.

Develop a support network that includes counselors, professors, tutors, and peers.

Schedule regular meetings with the aforementioned network.

Attempt to match students with accommodating professors.

Discuss any sensitivities to light or sound, or other needs.

Socialize with others who have similar interests.

Join club(s) that are exciting.

REFERENCES

Ganz, J. B., Earles-Vollrath, T. L., & Cook, K. E. (2011, July/August). Video modeling: A visually based intervention for children with autism spectrum disorder. *Teaching Exceptional Children, 43*(6), 8–18.

Hensley, P. (2012). 22 tips for teaching students with autism spectrum disorders. *Teaching Community.* Retrieved from http://teaching.monster.com/benefits/articles/8761.

Hutton, M. (2012, January). 40 tips for parenting defiant teens with Asperger syndrome. *My Aspergers Child.* Retrieved from http://www.myaspergerschild.com/2012/01/40-tips-for-pa-renting-defiant-teens.html.

Meadan, H., Ostrosky, M. M., Triplett, B., Michna, A., & Fettig, A. (2011, July/August). Using visual supports with young children with autism spectrum disorder. *Teaching Exceptional Children, 43*(6), 28–35.

Moreno, S. J. (n.d.) Tips for teaching high-functioning people with autism. *Online Asperger Syndrome Information and Support @ Minnesota Association of Alternative Programs.* Retrieved from http://www.aspergersyndrome.org/Articles.

Morrison, J. Q., Sansosti, F. J., & Hadley, W. M. (2009). Parent perceptions of the anticipated needs and expectations for support for their college-bound students with Asperger's syndrome. *Journal of Postsecondary Education and Disability, 22*(2), 78–87.

Ontario Ministry of Education. (2012). Helpful tips for parents and caregivers of elementary school students. *Parents* (brochure). Retrieved from http://www.edu.gov.on.ca/eng/ document/brochure/tips.html.

Chapter 5

Daniel's Story

OHI—Attention Deficit Hyperactivity Disorder

Daniel is a young man who was diagnosed in elementary school with having attention deficit disorder (ADD). This neurologically based disorder meant that he displayed an inability to pay attention that was manifested by fidgeting, being easily distracted, incomplete work, excessive talking, blurting out in class, and interrupting others. Additionally, he had difficulty processing information, making decisions, solving problems, and self-regulating. A study conducted by the National Institute of Mental Health suggests that ADD results from a chemical imbalance in certain neurotransmitters that are responsible for regulating behavior. Essentially, the rate at which the brain uses glucose, the brain's main font of energy, is lower in people who have ADD.

Daniel's best recollection of when he first started having issues with focusing and staying on task was when he was retained by his mother in the fifth grade. In one particular class, Daniel was experiencing an immense amount of boredom. To counter this, he would often tell this teacher he had to use the restroom. He would disappear for long periods of time because he was making bubbles and entertaining himself by blowing on them.

One day Daniel's teacher looked for and found him playing in the restroom. He was very angry that Daniel was wasting time rather than working on his academic subjects. This teacher conferred with the principal, who called Daniel's mother and accused Daniel of masturbating while in the bathroom. Daniel states that at ten years of age, he did not even know what this was. He asserts he was entertaining himself in the bathroom for a long period of time because his work was easy for him, so he would complete it quickly and avoid boredom by engaging in an activity that he found interesting. Daniel believes that what happened next is that his work was reviewed, his teachers realized he understood grade-level material, and the decision was made to promote him to the sixth grade. Thus, he moved from the elementary school to the middle school environment.

Daniel remembers being singled out by his classmates when he was in elementary school. In fact, he felt like an outcast all the way through high school. Even today he describes himself as a loner with his best friend being his dad. The only successful interaction he recalls is playing wall ball (akin to the game of tag but with a ball). Otherwise, he recalls having plenty of fights in elementary school.

The combination of his fights, the fact that he was a loner, and his resistance to do work as evidenced by the time spent in the bathroom resulted in his being identified as "trouble." He was therefore tested and, he recalls, initially identified as ADD. He believes it was later that his diagnosis was changed to attention deficit hyperactivity disorder (ADHD). His mother was the one who explained to him that this meant he was overactive and excessively hyper. He does not recall having his exceptionality being described to him by any educators or other professionals at school.

Upon the individualized education program (IEP) team's decision to promote him to the sixth grade, Daniel recalls that it was his mother who explained that this sudden promotion was occurring because his teachers realized he was too smart for the fifth grade. Daniel states, "I could see right past that explanation." He remembers that he was told the class he would be entering would be smaller with more one-on-one assistance with someone who was readily accessible to help him instead of having a teacher working with twenty-five other students. He does not believe that being placed into the smaller, self-contained environment was helpful. Instead, he felt this isolated him from the rest of the students in the school. "I felt singled out once again, even though by this time I was rather used to this feeling." He recalls internally feeling "very crappy over the whole situation."

Because he hated school so much, his memory of middle school is that "I created hell the whole time." Specifically, he remembers the time his self-contained teacher attempted to move him into a regular education English class in the middle of the semester. He acted out and refused to cooperate with his English teacher, thus ensuring that he would be brought back to the self-contained environment. He states that his reasoning was that "it was awkward to walk into a classroom midsemester that had already been in session; I felt like an outsider—the black sheep walking in and everybody staring at me making me feel out of place once again." His suggestion for teachers is to wait for a more appropriate time, such as semester break, to place a student in another classroom. He also believes that this should be done on a trial basis to ensure that the new placement is a good fit for both the student and the teacher.

Daniel remembers being upset when he was told he was going to be in "special education." He recalls yelling at somebody, stating, "Why am I in special education? I'm not dumb; I'm not stupid, so why am I being placed in here?" He does have a vague recollection of someone's explaining to him that he was correct and that he did have normal intelligence. He remembers someone saying, "Daniel, you're not stupid—we don't think that. We're just putting you in this class to help you out." Beyond this statement, Daniel does not remember much about middle school.

Daniel believes he had most of his classes in the general education environment in seventh and eighth grade with some classes in the self-contained environment. He liked being mainstreamed rather than being cooped up in a carrel. He remembers being successful and enjoying classes such as home economics (cooking) and photography. However, he also remembers his general education teachers' permitting him to go to the library frequently for the purpose of having a quiet place to work. In reality, he was unsupervised and entertained himself on the computer by playing games instead of doing his work. This accommodation was clearly ineffective.

Daniel does not remember being involved in any IEP meetings except for the one that occurred his senior year. He was exited from special education services at that time. He remembers being asked by the adults in the room if he believed he was ready to leave the special education program, and he responded that he felt more than ready. Although he was attending some general education classes, he felt overwhelmed when his special education resource (pullout) classes were immediately replaced with general education courses, especially because he missed material that had already been taught.

"Overall, I felt relieved to be out of the special education environment and not thought of as being 'retarded' by my peers, although it was tough academically." He knew he had to buckle down and work hard if he was going to be able to graduate at the end of the year. In retrospect, Daniel wonders if being exited was imposed on him because the consequence of being exited his senior year is that it has prevented him from receiving support and resources in the postsecondary environment, for example, college scholarships, grants, and being able to collaborate with organizations that support students who receive services. "I feel screwed because I have had to pay for everything out of pocket up to this point and have received no assistance."

Daniel took Ritalin when he was initially identified as ADD. He recalls sitting in class and feeling mentally numb. He was supposed to be able to focus better, but it was almost as if the reverse were true; he felt "out of it" and unable to concentrate. He eventually told his mother that he did not feel right, so his doctor prescribed Prozac. Shortly thereafter, he told his mother that he was not going to take any more medication. He confesses that in his mind Prozac was for "crazy people." He thought this because he knew some-body who was on Prozac who could not control himself, had mood swings, and exhibited off-the-wall behavior.

Daniel does not recall being on medication in high school. He states that he was able to focus, but he did so only in classes he liked. He describes this as "a pick-and-choose situation. When I wasn't doing well it was actually an act of rebellion." When he did rebel, he was sent to in-school suspension (ISS) for the designated number of days and then returned to class. "This happened frequently, but I did not mind because I was merely missing a class I did not care about anyway."

In reality, it worked well for both him and the teacher; he was out of a class that he hated and the teacher was not being interrupted. He confesses he was placed in ISS because he told the teacher to screw off, threw spit wads, and engaged in other childlike behavior. He thinks he did this because he hated school. He remembers being in trouble a lot. He never took notes during class because he felt they did not matter and he did not care. He now wonders whether he was trying to avoid work or get attention.

During his high school years, Daniel's friends were mostly girls. Thus, he liked his weight class because it "made me buff." He also liked weights because he did not have to perform every exercise because he had an issue with his back. He was therefore able to focus on building his biceps. He believes he was able to get rid of some of his anger and use up some of his energy. Regretfully, his weight teacher did not provide instruction or assis-tance. Instead, he had a chart on the wall and expected his students to read and follow its guidelines.

While in high school, Daniel attended study hall. This class consisted only of special education students and the room had partitions. He does not know if he was in this class because it was an accommodation written in his IEP. He also remembers frequent testing in high school. He does not recall if he was separated from his general education peers during test time because testing occurred with many others in the cafeteria. He did not realize tests had any importance because no one told him they did.

Nor did Daniel realize that his grades mattered. It was not until he submit-ted his transcript at college that he recognized there was some importance to them. He was surprised to learn he had passed the state test required by the No Child Left Behind Act (NCLB) because he was not serious about it. He does not remember receiving any accommodations but realizes he may have. He does not believe standardized tests accurately measure one's ability or determine his or her future success.

An active Eagle Scout, Daniel was sexually abused by a scout leader when in the tenth grade. The abuser went to jail for only ninety days, was required to register as a sex offender, had his certification as a scout leader revoked, and was released back into the community. The trauma resulted in

Daniel's meeting with multiple psychiatrists, but he does not believe they helped him. After this event the fights he got into were intense—once he started fighting he couldn't stop. In his mind, he was taking revenge on the man who had physically violated him.

This perpetrator still lives in Daniel's town, so Daniel sees him and his brother frequently. The desire for revenge is still strong; it has taken a lot of self-control to not go after the offender. Daniel states that he still gets angry that this one person has adversely affected him for so many years. Now that he has his own family, he has tried to put the incident in the past and move on. He believes staying busy helps him deal with the pain. He refuses to let his own children be involved in scouting because he would not be able to protect them every minute. His choice is to take the high road.

Regarding postsecondary goals, Daniel was interested in the culinary arts and respiratory therapy. Even though he was exited from special education services his senior year, he does not recall having a discussion with any special education teacher, case worker, or school counselor regarding these goals in ninth, tenth, or eleventh grade. No course work, contact with outside agencies, or objectives were put into place to help him obtain his transition goals. He believes tuition should result in receiving a salary that reflects the financial investment and effort required from the student, and one should not have to "settle" for less. Because tuition at the schools he has researched appears to exceed the salary he believes he would subsequently receive, he has currently discarded his plans to attend a culinary arts school or academic program for a respiratory therapy certificate.

In terms of education, Daniel does not believe there is anything more his teachers could have done to help him. He states that the onus was on him, and many issues arose due to his attitude. He does remember having days when he woke up thinking, "This is going to be a great day. I am going to get all my work done." Ultimately, however, he was not able to make it happen.

He muses that if he is really interested in something, he can focus and complete a task. Now that he has graduated and works full-time, he is always busy and productive, which is not how he was while in school. He speculates that a traditional classroom environment was not conducive to his being successful because he could not sit and concentrate for long periods of time. He likes to be busy and active with hands-on activities. He thinks that perhaps if he had had large chunks of the day with hands-on activities doing tasks he liked, school might have been more enjoyable. After reflecting a bit, Daniel maintains that he perceived school as boring, and he does not believe there was anything more that could have been done to keep him interested. The best time of day was when the dismissal bell rang, freeing him from the bondage of the educational environment.

Daniel acknowledges that some teachers have a particular enthusiasm that can make a boring subject tolerable. Teachers whom he enjoyed were his choir teacher and a special education teacher who taught him in a class that required an extensive amount of writing. This writing teacher would give him prompts and help stimulate his mind before he was asked to complete a task. He took choir only in his senior year and regrets that he did not know how much fun it could be when he first entered high school. He remembers performing in a concert and acting and dancing. Those two teachers' attitudes helped move him forward.

Conversely, he had a college teacher who was so terrible that the highest grade in the class was about 40 percent. She therefore informed the class that she was going to give everybody twenty "free" points. Daniel speculates this was so she could make herself look good and keep her job.

A suggestion Daniel has is for teachers to be willing to be flexible and try to understand that students can find the solution to a problem if given time; there is more than one creative way to analyze a problem. Teachers also need to praise students for their successes. His biggest obstacle to enjoying school was the narrow-minded negative attitude teachers appeared to have regarding problem solving. He admits he contributed to the problem because he was hotheaded, but he believes he showed that side of himself only when somebody first behaved poorly toward him.

Daniel believes that improving the education system requires more than one person's addressing any issue to effect change. To parents and students who deal with ADD, he suggests that students take their medication. He also suggests staying busy as a crucial strategy to keep life from falling apart. He recommends creating a daily agenda; he does so in his head instead of writing it down. He firmly believes no one knows what tomorrow holds, so it is important to live day by day. He therefore sets short-term goals which include fulfilling responsibilities along with enjoyable hobbies. "Life is tough—take it day by day."

Daniel says the best thing that has happened to him since he left high school is marrying his wife and having his kids. He believes any successes he has had as a husband or father is due to the modeling provided by his parents. "Otherwise, nothing can prepare one for parenthood—it is trial and error." He currently lives near his parents and works in the family business as his day job. He does not particularly like it because it involves a lot of labor.

Daniel immensely enjoys trapping and would like to learn taxidermy. He describes trapping as a major adrenaline rush "because catching an animal by the ankle takes a special kind of talent." Although trapping started out as a hobby, it has evolved into a passion that he would like to turn into a commercial business. He has a great business mind and knows how to work hard, build a clientele, and make money. With his fingers in many pies, he is clearly enjoying life and successfully conquering his challenges.

TIPS FOR TEACHERS OF ATTENTION DEFICIT HYPERACTIVITY DISORDERED STUDENTS

- Get the student's attention before giving directions.
- Maintain eye contact during verbal instruction.
- Slow your presentation speed.
- Prompt the student to repeat instructions.
- Use visual aids to illustrate verbal information.
- Seat student in quiet area away from windows, doors, pencil sharpeners, and trash cans.
- Increase distance between desks.
- Assign fewer items.
- Talk less and do more.
- Switch between high-interest and low-interest tasks.
- Break one task into smaller, more manageable parts to be completed at different times.
- Allow extra time for work completion.
- Use a timer.
- Actively involve the student in the lesson.
- Establish behavioral expectations prior to the questioning period.
- Clarify ground rules.
- Cue students before asking questions.
- Ensure that 75 percent of the questions produce a positive or accurate response.
- Ask follow-up questions.
- Permit ear phones or ear plugs to block distractions during seat work.
- Reinforce through praise.
- Allow the student to have an extra set of books at home.
- Organize desk.
- Provide a printed schedule.
- Alternate short work periods with frequent breaks.
- Establish a secret signal to indicate the child is off task.
- Create a list to help organize and prioritize tasks.
- Ensure that material has the appropriate level of difficulty.
- Provide hands-on activities.
- Teach the lesson at a brisk pace.
- Highlight main ideas.
- Create worksheets with a lot of white space.

TIPS FOR STUDENTS WITH ATTENTION DEFICIT HYPERACTIVITY DISORDER

- Use a planner and schedule everything in it.
- Create specific, measurable goals.
- Break big tasks down to smaller ones that are specific and measureable, for example, if you must read fifty pages in a week, read ten pages per night.
- Structure regular breaks by using a timer, for example, work for thirty minutes, break for ten minutes.
- Reward yourself when you have accomplished a goal.
- Use review sheets, handouts, and classroom assignments to prepare for tests.
- Clarify the chapters and main topics that will be tested.
- Be proactive by sharing your ADHD symptoms and issues with your teacher.
- Partner with an organized person.
- Find a study area free of distractions.
- Create flashcards or outlines.
- Join a study group if it is organized and focused.
- Use mnemonics to help you remember information, for example, the mnemonic for the planets is My Very Earnest Mother Just Served Us Nine Pickles: Mercury, Venus, Earth, Mars, Jupiter, Saturn, Uranus, Neptune, Pluto.
- Exercise.
- Highlight important information.
- Place sticky notes pointing to important information.
- Ask for help—everyone needs to at different times.

REFERENCES

Bettenhausen, S. (1998). Surviving the student with ADHD. *Teaching Excellence Newsletter sponsored by Eastern New Mexico University.*

Bolyn, M. (2010, March 15). Techniques for ADHD students. *Livestrong.com.* Retrieved from http://www.livestrong.com/article/93860-techniques-adhd-students/.

Bond, N. B. (2008, February). Questioning strategies that minimize behavior problems. *Education Digest, 73*(6), 41–45.

Fowler, M. (2010, October). Increasing on-task performance for students with ADHD. *Education Digest, 76*(2), 44–50.

Low, K. (2010, April 13). Exam study tips for students with ADHD. *About.com Health's Disease and Condition.* Retrieved from http://add.about.com/od/schoolissues/a/Exam-Study-Tips.htm.

Tartakovsky, M. (2011). A toolkit for school success: 15 study tips for students with ADHD. *Psych Central*. Retrieved from http://psychcentral.com/lib/2011/a-toolkit-for-school-success-15-study-tips-for-students-with-adhd/2/.

Chapter 6

Daniel's Mother's Story

Attention Deficit Hyperactivity Disorder

Daniel's third-grade teacher contacted his mother several times throughout the school year to discuss his impulsive classroom behavior and inability to focus. His mother was told that he was not listening, failed to finish tasks he started, was easily distracted, could not seem to concentrate, and was always "on the go." These issues were interfering with his ability to problem solve and successfully complete his academic tasks. During one call, Mother was told that Daniel had gone into the restroom and had pooped in the trash can.

His inability to attend to any given situation beyond a few seconds and his tendency to engage in inappropriate behaviors continued through the fourth grade. The psychologist therefore screened him and determined he had attention deficit hyperactivity disorder (ADHD). When Mother was first told this and the exceptionality was described to her, she did not believe what she heard. Having been around boys all her life, she believed neither that excessive energy was unusual nor that it could be severe enough to interfere with one's ability to be academically successful. She walked away from her meeting with the psychologist believing she could "fix Daniel." She did not think what she heard was a big deal and that "it was just who Daniel was."

Mother believed an herbal approach would make Daniel better. She used an herb book to help guide her decisions; she began by giving him herbs such as L-lysine to slow him down. She collaborated frequently with Daniel's teacher to ascertain whether or not the herb therapy was having a positive effect on her son's behavior or ability to focus. His grades were not horrible, but he continued to have difficulty concentrating.

Ultimately, herbal therapy did not help him, so Mother acquiesced and when he was in fifth grade, took him to the doctor to get prescription medicine. She was resistant to putting him on the recommended medicine, Ritalin, but eventually complied with his doctor's recommendation. As a way to address her concerns about overmedicating her son with Ritalin, she would not give him his dose after school, during weekends, or over holidays. This strategy appeared to work.

Although Daniel passed the fifth grade, Mother chose to have him repeat the year so he could mature. One day she received a phone call requesting her presence at a meeting. Upon entering the conference room she was astonished to see the number of people, many of whom she did not know, and wondered why so many people were there. "It was clear to me that this was going to be a terrible meeting."

After introductions were made, a teacher accused Daniel of masturbating in the bathroom (the truth was that he was playing with the soap and making bubbles). This devastating accusation "hit me like a ton of bricks. I believe if Daniel had been in an appropriate classroom with more engaging hands-on activities he would have been more interested in school." This volatile meeting felt extremely antagonistic as each teacher described Daniel's disruptive behavior. The meeting culminated in a team decision to promote Daniel to the sixth grade so he could be placed in the middle school's self-contained classroom.

Initially upset, Mother now believes this decision saved him. She states that the compassionate, loving feeling she received from the sixth-grade teacher who was going to work with Daniel was the deciding factor in her choice to agree to the placement. The program he was going to enter was described to her, and it sounded significantly more positive than what he was currently experiencing. She also believes the animosity his fifth-grade teachers were displaying influenced her decision. Mother still asserts that ultimately the person who has had the biggest impact on his life was this sixth-grade teacher of the self-contained class because this class was the first time Daniel experienced any praise in the school environment.

Mother believes the individualized education program (IEP) plan that placed Daniel in the self-contained classroom was appropriately written and that it supported him by implementing practical instructional strategies. "Daniel was never happier with school than his sixth-grade year. It was a real change for him to come home from school in a good mood. Prior to this, he did not care about school at all. Being in a predictable, consistent, fair class seemed to make all of the difference in the world. From sixth grade on he had a much better life."

Mother does not remember IEP meetings in middle school (seventh and eighth grades). She remembers Daniel was mainstreamed and classes went well for him. She recalls receiving phone calls only a few times for issues that were quite insignificant when compared to those in elementary school.

Mother was the only family member who attended the IEP meetings. This sometimes felt overwhelming as the weight of making decisions fell squarely on her shoulders. When she attended meetings, she did not understand the language or what was on the printed page. She had to trust that what she was signing was what she was told was in the IEP packet and was in the best interest of her child. She does not feel she asked the right questions throughout the years because she did not know what those questions were. She would advise other parents that if they wish to successfully navigate the education system, they should research the IEP process on the Internet or ask other parents. She wishes she had known more about her rights as a parent and about the process.

Prior to his placement in special education, Daniel did not have very many friends. He was belittled even though he knew how to stand up for himself. After he was labeled as "special ed.," his social life declined even more. He was frequently made fun of, a situation he really hated. He begged his mother for years to get him out of special education, but she encouraged him to stay to receive the help he needed. It was indeed a very exciting day for him when as a high school senior he was finally exited from services.

When Daniel went to high school, he was in all mainstream classes. He had accommodations such as books on tape, the use of the computer, and other accommodations to help him with tests. These accommodations were made available to him but he did not necessarily use them. He hated math but passed the class.

An Eagle Scout, Daniel was sexually abused by his scout master when he was in the tenth grade. This was devastating to him. Due to his anger rages, he was put on Prozac, a prescription he took until his junior or senior year. (Mother speculates that he could perhaps occasionally still benefit from this prescription.) In retrospect, it appears that his sudden onsets of rage probably came from this incident. The silver lining is that the incident has probably helped him become a better father because he knows he does not want his children to go through what he did.

Daniel loves to cook and wanted to attend culinary school. Mother does not recall his being offered any transition advice prior to being exited from special education his senior year. She wondered why he was offered the option to exit services—she felt as if he still could have used the help. Even though Daniel wanted out of special education, she felt as if he had already been labeled, so being exited his senior year was not going to have a positive impact. She did understand that from his perspective, he was no longer going to be viewed as "different." She knew he had low self-esteem and thought that exiting him might improve his view of himself.

Mother states that during the exit meeting, it was made clear to Daniel what the consequences of exiting were going to be. She felt he made a hasty decision due to his negative self-perception. As a parent she knew he needed the help and believed he would have a better life after high school if he continued to receive services. However, that was not what he wanted. It was very tough for her to permit him to make this decision, and she emphasized that he would not be able to have resource help any longer. He was adamant that he wanted to be exited.

Mother believes that by the time a student is in high school, especially near the end, he or she has his or her own mind and perspective. She believes if a child chooses to exit special education, "the parent needs to step back and let them experience the consequences of their choice—both good and bad. Allowing them to make their own choices empowers them and improves their self-esteem." Her experience is that a student matures and grows in the area of self-esteem long after he or she leaves school. "Maturation comes with time. Students therefore need free agency to make decisions. After giving a student all of the information possible, the decision is ultimately theirs."

Mother does not recall if Daniel was separated from his general education peers during the state testing required by the No Child Left Behind Act (NCLB), but speculates that he was. She does know that he did not care about the test. Mother believes schools test too much in general, but especially as testing relates to special education students. "Special education students need to be tested at the level at which they are working."

Mother believes that current tests are unreasonably long. "There is no way a student with ADHD can pass the test because it requires too much reading and focus at one time." She does not feel it is fair for students to be required to pass standardized tests in order to graduate because the tests often do not apply to the needs or interests of the students. She proudly notes that Daniel did successfully pass the state test and all his courses, and graduated.

Daniel's mother advises other parents of children with ADHD to minimize the label or to try to keep other students from knowing their child is in the special education program. She knows this could be difficult but believes inclusion is one positive step in helping the children develop friendships. "It is difficult for special education children to interact with their friends on the playground or during breaks and then be segregated when they have to return to class. Students who participate in more activities and are included in the student body to a greater extent have greater self-esteem."

Mother states that the worst thing a school can do to interfere with special education students' success is to prevent them from interacting with their peers. Honoring the principle of least restrictive environment is paramount. She says that having something like a study hall room with staff available to assist as needed is important. It is also comforting to have a safe haven when needed. After decompressing, the student should be able to return to the classroom. This program should be available to general education and special education students alike.

Mother says the best thing that has happened to Daniel since he left high school is getting married. Although he still has bouts of rage, he loves and cares deeply for his wife and children. "His daughter has really softened him. He is nicer to his wife and sons since her birth. He is more willing to openly show affection."

When Daniel graduated from high school, he worked in the family business as well as for a paint company, where he discovered he had a talent in this trade. He learned the importance of hard work and is willing to invest all of himself. He also discovered he had talents for trapping, cooking, gardening, working with honey bees, and gold prospecting. He develops goals in his head and follows through with them.

Although it took a long time for Daniel to know in his mind what he needed to do, what path he needed to be on, and how to channel his energies, he knows his hard work is making him successful. He has taken his dreams and turned them into accomplishments. He is active in his church and does everything that he is asked to do. He is very responsible now and prioritizes his responsibilities. He thinks of others before himself. Mother speculates that he may have been selfish initially because he was not receiving what he needed from others earlier in life.

TIPS FOR PARENTS OF STUDENTS WITH ATTENTION DEFICIT HYPERACTIVITY DISORDER

- Remember that your child's misbehavior is not intentional.
- Praise and positively reinforce small accomplishments.
- Seek support and advice from doctors, teachers, therapists, and support groups.
- Establish a routine that is predictable, including bedtime.
- Set timers to signal transition time, for example, end of bath time and dressing for bedtime.
- Post a schedule including tasks and free time.
- Create a quiet, private space where your child can concentrate.
- Model neatness by showing that everything has a place.

- Keep your child busy but avoid overscheduling activities that will result in the child's being overwhelmed.
- Display a chart with stickers, smiley faces, or points that visually remind your child what appropriate, positive behavior looks like.
- Provide multiple opportunities for movement.
- Find a sport or activity your child enjoys and minimize time in front of the television.
- Use a calming scent or relaxation tapes in your child's room.
- Visit parks or walking trails.
- Avoid fatty, sugary foods.
- Role-play different social situations.
- Invite only one or two peers to play with your child at one time.

REFERENCE

Smith, M., & Segal, J. (2011, June). ADD/ADHD parenting tips: Helping children with attention deficit disorder. *Helpguide Harvard Health Publications.* Retrieved from http://helpguide.org/ mental/adhd_add_parenting_strategies.htm.

Chapter 7

Howard's Story

Dyslexia

Howard is a recent college graduate who has excelled as a learner with dyslexia. Dyslexia is an impairment in the brain that affects one's ability to translate written images into meaningful language because letters and words get jumbled. Students with dyslexia are often very bright, but their intellectual abilities go unnoticed as they are slow to learn words and often write words and/or letters backward. Specific teaching methods are needed to address these students' perceptual and processing difficulties.

Howard first noticed that something was not right when he was having trouble keeping up with his classmates in reading. His concerned dad would attempt to help him read words on flash cards, but he was not successful. He helplessly struggled with simple words and phrases such as "Bob sat" or "Tom sat." At that time, he was tested and diagnosed as a student with a learning disability in reading. In subsequent years, he received the same diagnosis; thus, his teachers realized he had difficulty with reading but they did not recognize that he specifically had dyslexic issues. Subsequently, he struggled, was frustrated, and felt embarrassed. He believed there was a reason for his academic difficulties and therefore a solution, but he didn't know what that nameless solution was or how to find it.

Beginning in first grade, Howard also had trouble with math, and he states to this day, as a proud college graduate, that he still struggles with the elusive subject. His teachers noted he could do tasks better orally and visually on paper rather than in his head (although his writing was illegible), so he was provided with a keyboard to type his words. Howard saw himself as intelligent, and his mother also believed he was bright, so both were at a loss as to why he was not doing well in school.

His inability to successfully complete even the simplest academic tasks led to faculty and staff members' thinking he was lazy, he wasn't smart, and that he had attention deficit disorder (ADD). Unctuous doctors put him on various medicines such as Ritalin and Concerta, which worked to an extent because he could hyperfocus, but since ADD was not his issue, the drug's positive effects were minimal. He took an IQ test at an early age but remembers having difficulty sitting through the lengthy test because he was so young. Thus, faculty, staff, and administrators from when he was in kindergarten through eighth grade "just thought I was lazy."

Howard never had a traditional individualized education program (IEP) because he always attended private school. As an alternative, his teachers, administrators, someone from the learning lab, and parents would gather in small meetings and discuss how they could help him. From kindergarten through fifth grade, he was not included in the conversation. The adults would talk for about ten minutes, assure his parents that he was in a good school, and send everybody on their way. No one ever looked over at him during these mundane meetings or asked him how he felt: "It was as if I was invisible."

Howard's accommodations included being able to orally answer questions and being able to type answers for class work and exams on the computer. However, these essential accommodations were not consistently implemented as some teachers were not as understanding as others. Thus, some teachers did not permit these accommodations. The lack of consistency caused Howard to adamantly believe that no one cared. This resulted in a terrible school experience. He felt as though he were a helpless slave in a heartless system, being made fun of with no one asking him how he felt or trying to help him.

Resource class felt like a joke, as it consisted of being babysat while playing for an hour on PlayStation with mindless video games or with cards. Getting up to leave his general education class for his resource class was embarrassing because all his classmates watched him leave. He felt he was simply being pushed aside, slipping by because nobody wanted to make the assertive effort required to help him succeed. Even though he was young, this pullout approach was puzzling. He was frustrated because he wanted to be with his classmates instead of playing a game in an isolated room and feeling embarrassed. He recognized this as a typical trend for younger students with dyslexia. To clarify, Howard understood that being sent to resource class for the right reasons was worth the embarrassment, but being sent to play cards or video games was not that right reason.

Beginning in fifth grade, Howard attended a different school. He was reading at the first-grade level. He believed he was smart, but he was unable to act on his intelligence. School was rough because he would attend class and try his best, but he could not perform his tasks due to the lack of support and specialized instruction to meet his needs. At that time, his classes were separated into the low, middle, and high groups. Everyone was assured there was no difference, but Howard could clearly tell there was by the sarcasm in the teacher's voice. He felt isolated when he was placed in the low class because it consisted of very few students, and his friends were in the high class.

Howard did not have to take the state standardized test because he attended a private school. Still, he hated the tests he had to take for his classes. In these formative years, he usually tested in the same room as his peers. He despised sitting in the same room as his many classmates because there were too many distractions such as noise or movement—he would fail instantly if there were any. He was supposed to have the option of testing in a separate room and be permitted double the time to complete his test, but he never received this accommodation. He often left the test blank, staring out the window instead, because he saw no point in even trying.

Consequently, his grades were abysmal. If he tried to answer the questions, he felt rushed and was rarely able to finish his test on time. This contributed to his being called lazy. He stresses that having extra time can make all of the difference in the world—not having time as an accommodation can be tough for those with dyslexia.

Socially, Howard didn't have as much time at lunch as his general education classmates. Furthermore, he had few classmates to sit with because his high-performing friends were discussing what they needed to do to get ready for their next class and he didn't fit into that substantive conversation. Therefore, he would sit with a few of his kindred, sequestered classmates in "the low class." During recess, his cacophonic peers made fun of him and pointed at him, calling him "the loser" or "the stupid one." Consequently, he became introverted, not wanting to expose himself to more insidious pain. The experience had a "tangible negative effect, wasn't fun, and was quite depressing." Howard was fortunate, however, because he was a big kid, in great shape, and good at sports, which prevented his being bullied; sports were the one arena in which he was triumphant.

Howard recalls only one teacher who was nice to him between first and eighth grade. He is not sure why she was nice and speculates it was because she felt sorry for him. Conversely, he remembers an incident in middle school in which his teacher made fun of him when he drew a stick figure but didn't put a face on it. He also recalls that his French teacher would not allow him to go to the bathroom until he got an answer right. Due to his language difficulties as a result of his dyslexia, he had significant trouble speaking English and even greater difficulty with French. Learning French was torture. So, he did little work because he "hated that class."

Similarly, his eighth-grade English teacher picked on him. If the class was doing an exercise with a word tree, she would wait until after the more simple items were worked through, and then she would call on him to read a phrase that was clearly far beyond his ability. This English teacher would subsequently tell his parents that he was stupid. His parents adamantly disagreed and said they were going to get him tested somewhere else.

Howard had very low self-esteem because almost 100 percent of his teachers had told him he was stupid and he eventually bought into their denigrating statements. As a result, Mom had to drag him out of bed, fighting with him every day to go to school. He didn't want to go to school and when he did, he would often go hide and cry in the bathroom. He preferred to sit in the repugnant bathroom and cry than get called on and be embarrassed in his classes. Consequently, he was punished for hiding and not being in class.

Howard eventually became depressed because he was so fiercely miserable. He notes that he sometimes didn't care if he was alive. "I thought if I was dead, I would be better off." He posits that many students with dyslexia have this feeling, which goes undiagnosed and therefore unaddressed. He comments that "the good news is when kids are little they can't drive and can do very little about their low feelings."

Howard's parents knew he was unhappy and depressed. They tried everything to help him feel better, from taking him to see various specialists, including psychologists, to buying him toys. None of the strategies worked beyond being a temporary fix. If he was at Toys"R"Us and received something he really liked, he would have a few hours of happiness, but the deep internal issue was not resolved, so he would become deeply depressed again. His psychologists did not recognize the problem and said he had ADD that rendered him unable to focus.

Between eighth and ninth grade, Howard's parents, resolute in their goal to ensure that he received the best education available, took him to a high school that specialized in dyslexia. He was tested and his dyslexia was correctly identified "in about five minutes." When this diagnosis occurred, Howard's issue was thoroughly explained to him. This permitted him to clearly understand what was wrong and that "I was not stupid."

Both he and his parents felt elated. His dad shared that Woodrow Wilson had dyslexia, as did Albert Einstein, Picasso, and many other great people. This was encouraging and made Howard feel as if he could clearly be successful with hard work. He describes his correct diagnosis as a "relief" and "a breath of fresh air" because someone had finally put an accurate name to his exceptionality. He always believed he was not lazy or stupid; he now knew he was going to finally have an enviable opportunity to excel, and he liked the feeling.

Howard had always had strong support at home and a great relationship with his parents, even prior to being diagnosed. He always felt that he could be very open with them, even from an early age. Now that he knew what he had and that other great men had been successful with the same diagnosis, he was inspired. Getting properly diagnosed made all his struggles up to that point come into focus. He was extremely grateful for his parents' willingness to relentlessly seek a correct diagnosis and setting that would accommodate his needs.

At his specialized high school, classes were small, with five to eight students in every classroom. In discussions before class, Howard's peers openly shared the same miserable story about their challenging experiences in education prior to attending this particular high school. Because everyone had the same exceptionality and similar experiences, no one was sitting in class laughing at anyone else's difficulties or questions. Howard realized that if he asked a perplexing question, probably half his classmates also did not understand the concept, so he was helping everyone.

Howard's high school had two programs: a preparatory program to pre-pare students for college and a remedial program. All students began in the remedial program. When he entered the ninth grade, Howard was reading at a second-grade level. Teachers began his remediation by implementing ap-propriate strategies such as using felt fabric so he could feel the shapes of letters with his fingers, feeling words in the mouth, writing in different col-ors, and learning to track from left to right.

High school was modeled after a military academy. Howard was always expected to be in the same school uniform with his shirt tucked in; otherwise, he would face a two-hour after-school detention. The academic day was very organized. In this program he had one tutor who met with all his teachers at least once a week. He met with this tutor for an hour every day. She was so skilled that it appeared she knew more about Howard than he knew about himself. She would say, "So, you have a science paper due on Wednesday," or "Your teacher said you weren't doing so well yesterday in her class. What's going on?"

This tutor would always have a daily agenda, but Howard was able to confidentially share his feelings about what was occurring with him and address that issue before beginning his academic work. His tutor therefore was viewed as his friend because she was adept at supporting him both socially and academically in the areas where he was struggling. She imple-mented best practices, doing whatever was needed to transfer information to him. Strategies included using a hands-on approach, acting a word out, visu-alizing his task before beginning to work on it, or having his math word problem explained to him in steps. These strategies "seemed to work like magic" and were so effective that although he entered ninth grade with a second-grade reading level, he left high school reading at the college level (an eleven-year gain accomplished in four years). He therefore appreciated the school's controlled environment that enabled him to focus.

Howard's teachers provided him with a great deal of attention and empowered him by imparting study skills, organizational skills, and other similar strategies so he could be successful in the world. One strategy they implemented was called "homework makeup." If Howard showed up to school without his homework, the school would make him contact his parents and tell them he was required to stay after school because he had not fulfilled his responsibility by completing his homework. This strict approach reinforced the fact that he was not being taught meaningless "stuff," contrary to his perception in his previous schools.

Howard's high school teachers met about once a month to review prior goals and set new ones for the following month. If these meetings were held without a parent present, the goals would be faxed home for Howard's parents' review and approval. In these meetings, Howard would be asked what goals he wanted to accomplish. He would state them, and they would be recorded. He would also complete a one-page paper stating what he had accomplished the previous month.

Howard felt good when he was asked about his goals. Discussing them prompted more buy-in into his education. On the other hand, he felt quite drained because he had so much to catch up on because his earlier misdiagnosis had stood in the way of his learning when he was younger. By the time he arrived home, he did not want to do homework. In spite of that, he forged ahead and started to see daily progress. This was encouraging because Howard is a results-driven individual.

Howard first noted progress after about three or four months. His teachers rewarded him for his efforts rather than for the results. Because the classes were so remedial, he had several opportunities to be praised throughout the day. He could see steady improvements, and his work improved as time went by, unlike in his earlier school years when he was not praised, but rather called stupid.

Howard's high school class was small and the strict rules of the school prevented other students from distracting him during tests. He could work in a separate room on a computer equipped with Word. His accommodations included being able to test in a separate room and having double the time to complete his exams. He also had this accommodation in college. (Similarly, he can receive this accommodation when taking tests like the Medical College Admission Test [MCAT] or Law School Admission Test [LSAT].) In high school, his classes were small enough that he usually did not need his own room. However, he did take the SAT in his own room with the time accommodation. He believes all students should take advantage of their accommodations.

Howard believes that standardized tests do not accurately portray what someone knows, but they do portray one's ability to take the type of test being administered. He sees no connection between standardized tests and real life and views the tests as a pointless exercise that does not get anyone anywhere. However, he recognizes that some requirements need to exist, so taking a test like the SAT may have its place. He does not believe standardized tests are the answer for someone to get a high school diploma or be admitted to college. He believes there is a better method but does not know what that alternative method might be.

When he was in high school, Howard always knew going to college was the best route (his parents made it clear that not going was not an option), and he clearly knew what he needed to do to attain that goal. He knew the application process was very competitive, and he had to get several recommendations and fill out applications. In the location where he was raised, most students initiated this process as high school sophomores. Likewise, he applied his sophomore year and was accepted to three schools by his junior year.

Howard's high school was not effective in transitioning him into the college environment. Except for his academic adviser's telling him about the need to self-declare (a university does not know an individual has a disability unless that individual chooses to disclose that information), he received no further assistance. Thus, nobody properly prepared him for issues one faces within the college environment, such as time management.

His university, however, did assist him as he specifically applied to the Strategic Alternative Learning Techniques (SALT) program. Howard describes SALT as his most positive academic experience after high school. This program is a student-centered model that provides comprehensive services including individualized educational planning and monitoring, tutoring, a computer lab, and workshops geared to meet the individuals' needs. He was permitted to schedule meetings with his Strategic Learning specialist whenever he felt the need. Participation in SALT maximized his success.

Howard's opinion is that the typical educator beats dyslexics down emotionally. "No matter how strong one is and how many skills one possesses, when they repeatedly beat you down, it hinders your success." He believes that words are more hurtful than people admit: "The saying 'Sticks and stones may break my bones but words will never hurt me' is untrue, and words do hurt immensely. Verbal abuse sticks, especially when you are young and impressionable."

The most negative experience at the university level occurred when an older professor told Howard he could not use his computer in class. When this professor was presented with a letter from the dean that said Howard could use the computer as an accommodation, the professor said OK, but he "didn't understand why [he] needed that." Howard describes the professor acting like "the order comes down from me, the king, and all of you peasants have to listen." When the professor said he didn't know why Howard needed the computer, Howard merely responded that it helped him. On another occasion, when a different professor said she didn't like computers, Howard said he would handwrite his notes and did so in an attempt not to make his need an issue.

Howard learned how to set realistic goals by observing the people around him. He had friends who became professional athletes, and he was able to observe the dedication and commitment it took (along with genetic attributes). Also, his parents and grandparents are professionals, and he recognized the hard work and sacrifices they had to make to be successful in their professions. He is a well-balanced young man who recognizes that wealth does not create happiness or self-esteem; rather, the hard work that brings well-earned self-satisfaction does.

The biggest influence that kept and still keeps Howard grounded is his parents. They encouraged him to do what he loved and what he was passionate about, not to work for the money because that does not buy happiness. He has already been successful in the sense that he has made a lot of money in business, but that has not changed the core of who he is. Yes, he may be able to buy luxury items, but he readily acknowledges that having expensive things does not make one happy. "While having a Ferrari does make life an amazing thing, it's the people in your life that make you happy."

Today, Howard occasionally gives speeches to others with dyslexia. His advice is to never give up. He believes that the one who succeeds is the one who holds on to the rope the longest, doesn't listen to what other people say, and doesn't let the words, behavior, and actions of others get to them. He advises students to impact their lives through their own chosen behavior and actions. He tells them to follow their dreams and that will make them successful. He also cautions them to remember that time flies.

When speaking to a group that includes teachers and students, he talks to the students first and then addresses the teachers at the conclusion of his presentation. He asks how many kids sit at their desks, bored and staring out the window watching squirrels carry acorns. It's a metaphor, but the story is the same for each dyslexic student: they are all bored and don't know what to do with their day. He encourages them to not give up and to be persistent even though others are telling them they are going to fail and are stupid. He encourages students to say no, they are not going to fail and they are going to prove the teachers wrong.

At the end of his presentation, he tells teachers to be compassionate and understanding. "If the student feels you are approachable, there can be a bond permitting the teacher to figure out what is going on." Furthermore, he advises teachers not to be overwhelmed by the number of students in their class. Teachers need to be aware that many students have dyslexia. Too many teachers seem to not care, a state that shuts students down. "Caring makes a difference."

When students ask Howard how they should decide what to do in life, he asks them what they enjoy doing in their spare time. "Lo and behold, they quickly see that what they like to do in their spare time is often something they can do as a career." He also tells them to ground themselves in reality. They have to know what is realistic.

Howard's current goals are to work within the technology industry with those he knows and trusts. He also would like to obtain an MBA at some future date. He knows some businesses pay for their employees to go to school. He also wants to be involved with supporting the dyslexic community.

Howard believes dyslexia is easy to diagnose when an astute specialist conducts the test. He feels it is a shame that so many students are undiagnosed or misdiagnosed. "The onus is on parents and educators to ensure that the proper tests are administered for the benefit of the student." He knows a successful doctor who told him that he had to work three times harder than everyone else in his class to succeed, but succeed he did. His final advice: "Don't be embarrassed and act like dyslexia is a disease or the plague."

TIPS FOR TEACHERS OF DYSLEXIC STUDENTS

Tips to Help Students in the Classroom

- Begin each lesson with a review of what has been taught.
- Provide an outline of new items to be taught.
- Print on colored paper to reduce glare.
- Boldface keywords.
- Create and implement a daily structured routine.
- Use folders and dividers.
- Break tasks down into small pieces of information.
- Provide handouts.
- Utilize demonstrations, observations, and experiments.
- Seat the student near the teacher for immediate assistance.
- Allow interaction with a peer helper.
- Teach to all modalities (oral, auditory, and kinesthetic).
- Praise often.
- Help students see their strengths.
- Learn with games whenever possible.
- Teach students to use logic instead of relying on memory.

- Be flexible.

Tips to Help Students When They Are Copying from the Blackboard

- Use different colors.
- Write words with adequate space between them.
- Provide time for the work to be copied from the board.

Tips to Help Students with Reading

- Introduce new words slowly and repeat them often.
- Ask the student to read at his or her current skill level.
- Match words to pictures.
- Permit the student to read separately with the teacher instead of aloud in the classroom.
- Provide reading material ahead of time for the student to practice.
- Provide recorded reading to enhance vocabulary.
- Model competent reading via paired or choral reading.
- Keep reading fun.

Tips to Help Students with Spelling

- Provide structured and systematic exposure to rules and patterns of language.
- Keep the structured list short.
- Include a few irregular words each week to improve free-writing skills.
- Teach proofreading.

Tips to Help Students with Mathematics

- Teach general mathematical terminology such as "add," "sum," "increase," and "total."
- Encourage the use of estimation.
- Allow the student to talk through each step of the problem.
- Permit the use of the addition and times-table squares.
- Use index cards to write keywords for reference.
- Practice learning mathematical vocabulary frequently.
- Highlight the decimal point in a different color.

Tips to Help Students with Handwriting

- Encourage writing in a cursive joined style.

- Examine a few words on the board and look for errors as a class.
- Provide a reference chart to assist with cursive script in upper- and lower-case.
- Practice handwriting using words the student understands.

Editing and Grading Student Work

- Give credit for effort and achievement.
- Grade creative writing according to context.
- Edit spelling mistakes according to ability.
- Include positive comments.
- Avoid using red pens to mark errors.
- Permit oral answers on class assignments, homework, and tests.

Technology Tips

- Record lectures.
- Videotape lessons and demonstrations.
- Use audiotaped versions of textbooks.
- Make interactive multimedia learning opportunities available.

Homework Tips

- Write homework assignments in the same place every day or provide handouts.
- Assign homework only if it benefits the student.
- Quietly assign less homework than what is expected of the students' peers.
- Ensure that homework items are written down accurately.
- Limit the time to be spent on homework.

Testing Tips

- Offer multiple-choice options or permit oral answers instead of requiring written short answers or essays.
- Read directions to the student.
- Allow extra time and rest breaks.

TIPS FOR PARENTS OF DYSLEXIC CHILDREN

Tips to Help Your Child with Reading

- If your child is young, read to him every day for ten minutes.

- Play sound games.
- Teach letter sounds from an early age.
- Teach high-frequency words such as "the," "is," and "then."
- Frequently ask your child what he just read.
- If your child encounters an unknown word, ask him to use context clues to guess its meaning.
- Use flash cards.
- Use tinted cellophane paper to minimize the difference between the black print and white page.
- Craft a new window from cardboard so your child sees only one line at a time.
- Break reading time into several small sessions.
- If your child is young, have him draw a picture of what he read.
- Begin with picture books that have few words.
- If your child is older, have him describe what he read.
- Play rhyming games.
- Take time to pronounce new words.
- Sing rhyming songs.
- Follow a simple recipe.
- Take your child shopping and have him get the different items from the list.
- Praise often.

Tips to Help Your Child with Writing

- Use Play-Do to make the shape of different letters.
- Write words in sand with your fingers.
- Do craft activities to learn different letters. For example, cut out a big *H* using cardboard and decorate it.
- Draw large letters on paper, place the paper on the floor, and step on the different letters.
- Match pictures that begin with the same letters.

Tips to Help Your Child with Mathematics

- Ensure that your child knows his numbers in order.
- Play games that require your child to count.
- Teach concepts in small steps.
- Make sure your child understands a concept before going on to the next one.
- Have your child draw his favorite numbers and signs.
- Allow the child to use a calculator.
- Use real coins and bills to teach money.

- Use objects such as stones or small toy animals to teach addition and subtraction.
- Use an abacus to teach counting.
- Teach circles, squares, and other shapes by asking children to collect or point at different objects.
- Arrange objects in order of size.
- Teach patterning using blocks, leaves, or pieces of colored paper.

Tips to Help Your Child with Homework

- Coordinate homework tasks with your child's teacher.
- Use graph paper to help your child keep math problems in line.
- Do not require perfection.
- Use books on tape to support your child's reading efforts.
- Incorporate multiple modalities when teaching a new skill.

TIPS FOR DYSLEXIC STUDENTS

- Self-advocate—know yourself, what you need, and how to get it.
- Be aware that 60 percent of students with dyslexia are also ADHD.
- The evaluation process is extensive and often includes an aptitude test, achievement test, memory test, and phonological processing test.
- Strive to know your strengths and skills—this will help you during your daily activities.
- Expect to receive multisensory instruction to improve your academic and speech skills.
- Interventions often include counseling and support groups.
- Request accommodations that help you such as books on tape, use of a calculator, extra time for tests, a spell checker, voice recognition software, and copies of the class lecture.
- Ask for modifications such as writing a two- instead of five-page report; note that this is possible only in K–12, not at the university level or when working for an employer.
- Seek supportive friends and adults who can help you not feel over-whelmed by the extra effort and treatment required to keep up with other students.

REFERENCES

Bailey, E. (2008, May 19). *Strategies for parents and their child with reading disabilities.* Retrieved from Eileen-bailey.suite101.com/helping-children-with-dyslexia.

Carbo, M. (2008, March). Best practices for achieving high, rapid reading gains. *Education Digest, 73*(7), 57–60.

Hodge, P. L. (2000). A dyslexic child in the classroom. Davis Dyslexia Association International, Dyslexia the Gift. Retrieved from http://www.dyslexia.com/ library/classroom.htm.

Johnson, N. (2011). *Self-advocacy: Know yourself, know what you need, know how to get it.* Retrieved from http://www.wrightslaw.com/info/sec504.selfadvo.ld.johnson.Htm.

McGraw-Hill Company (n.d.). Helping dyslexic students succeed. *Teaching Today.* Retrieved from http://teachingtoday.glencoe.com/ howtoarticles/helping-dyslexic-students-succeed.

Chapter 8

Mercedez's Story

Hearing Impairment

Mercedez is unclear as to when her hearing loss began. Her mother believes she never heard correctly because, from her very early years, Mercedez did not respond when spoken to; Mother would have to tap her to get her attention when inside or go into the yard to get her for dinner. Her father believes that when she was four she had an ear infection that caused her impairment. Her doctor explained that she had been born with a small eardrum and so the sound did not cause it to vibrate properly. The diagnosis is confusing because Mercedez was trilingual prior to age four; thus, she was hearing well enough to imitate speech when she was a toddler. After her diagnosis, Mercedez was fitted with hearing aids. Afterward, she noted that people began to treat her differently; for example, they spoke to her in only one language, English.

When Mercedez was enrolled in prekindergarten, she clearly recalls that it was a beautiful day when she met her teacher and played with her newfound friends and classmates. She began to receive special education services, was taught sign language, and participated in speech classes. She remembers being taught how to say the *s* sound in words such as "sweet" and "swim." In brief, Mercedez received services as soon as she was identified as a person with a hearing impairment.

After receiving her hearing aids, Mercedez remembers that her world turned into one that was alarmingly much louder. When she was in the car with her mom and dad, if a motorcycle passed, the noise would be so loud that the pain would make her cry. She begged for permission to take her hearing aids out, but her father insisted that she keep them in because they would ultimately benefit her. She did have a volume control but had great difficulty finding an acceptable setting that permitted her to hear but that did not hurt her.

Because she was so young, her friends easily accepted her. They did, however, have curious questions such as, "What's that in your ear?" They would want to touch her hearing aids and would ask if they could put them in their ears. Many students in her prekindergarten class also had hearing aids, a situation that helped her feel less out of place.

If someone made a comment questioning why she spoke differently, her mother explained that she had a hearing loss and requested that the other person be kind. Neither parent saw her as a person with a disability; rather, "they saw me as their lovely daughter who was perfect." When she went out into the world, others made accommodations. For example, at school her reading teachers would point to words and talk slowly. She asserts that speaking slowly was helpful if the concept being taught was difficult to understand; on the other hand, if the story was simple, reading slowly was annoying. Thus, reading slowly as an accommodation was useful and helpful if it occurred in the right context and at the correct level of difficulty.

Mercedez's parents divorced when she was four years old. She lived with her father for the next eight years. She went to the same elementary school and had the same special education teacher from kindergarten through sixth grade. She attended special education classes in the morning until lunchtime and then attended general education classes in the afternoon. In her morning classes, there were students with various disabilities; some were blind, some were deaf, and others had intellectual disabilities. During the morning, she would prelearn what was going to be taught in the afternoon. Her morning teacher taught every subject and would sign to her as she taught.

In her afternoon classes, her teachers would wear microphones that projected sound. She therefore did not need an interpreter with her in the afternoon unless there was a group activity. She liked her afternoon classes for three main reasons. First, there were more students in the classroom who were her neighborhood friends. Second, she was excited to get homework, "thinking it was a cool thing back in my younger days because I felt normal knowing that regular kids get homework too." Third, she wanted to learn the same material as the rest of the students in her regular education classes. Because of the tremendous, continuous support she received from her teachers, she always felt welcomed and as if she belonged.

As the years passed, Mercedez continued to receive speech services and study American Sign Language (ASL). She learned to speak quite well and thought learning to communicate with her hands and facial expressions, and through lipreading, "was really neat." She took advantage of her one-on-one time and blossomed. Yet she hated being labeled "special education" and believed her classes were too easy. "Every year seemed predictable and I didn't like knowing that I was 'special'; I mean, just because I am a bit different doesn't mean I should not learn like the rest of the students who aren't so different than me."

Even though she was just a young girl, Mercedez liked learning, participating in large groups, and doing fun activities with her hearing friends. What she didn't like about special education was her observation that some of the students were "let off easy." She believes all teachers should present challenging content that is appropriate for each student, and they should teach from their hearts. In her special education classes, she rarely had homework or needed to take notes, and she learned from alternative, easier material that stifled her progress. Additionally, she noticed that the students in her special education classes received inflated grades. "I remember when we would all take a test at the same time, though others had answers very different than mine; we all still received an A no matter what." She describes seeing multiple papers with different answers but the same high grade as "confusing."

Mercedez astutely noted that many students in the special education environment took advantage of their "special" setting. They did not apply themselves because they did not have to; by avoiding what was hard for them they became detrimentally "stuck in their comfort zone." An example is her fellow hearing-impaired classmates. Instead of learning society's English in addition to ASL, they liked ASL better because communicating with their hands was what they knew. Unfortunately, the way they sign is also the way they write, omitting verbs and adjectives that hearing people use, for example, "I'm go store" instead of "I'm going to the store."

When it came to reading, ASL students usually understood the concepts but often struggled with understanding why it was necessary to have so many additional words in the English language that were not in ASL; they were viewed as unnecessary. Thus, they didn't like being in regular education classes because English was very hard for them to understand, causing them to feel overwhelmed. Most did not wish to put forth the extra effort required to write like their hearing counterparts. Mercedez believes the extra effort was worth the payoff because "more doors are open if one knows how to properly communicate in the business world or in the general public arena."

In seventh grade, Mercedez moved to a junior high school. She was asked if she wanted to be in special education and she said no, she could do her work on her own. She felt she did not need anybody signing for her or talking to her slowly. She wanted to be treated like a regular education student.

She was very excited because she was able to take science, history, and Spanish classes with her friends. However, she did continue to receive speech services. She completed seventh grade on the honor roll. Everyone was very proud of her accomplishments, but no one was more proud than she was. She believes she was successful and independent because of the good foundation she received in her formative years.

At the end of seventh grade, Mercedez had a discussion with her father. She explained to him that she had lived with him for eight years and now, due to her changing body, she needed a mother's example in her life. She clarified that the request did not reflect negatively on him, that she loved him very much, and that she was grateful for the foundation he had given her. Rather, she felt the time had come to learn how to be a lady and establish a relationship with her mother. She explained she would live eight years with her mother and then live on her own. Her father was heartbroken, as any father would be, but understood and agreed. He told her he would always be there for her and she was welcome home anytime.

Mercedez moved to another state to live with her mother as she began eighth grade. The transition was very difficult because she had no friends and was in a very different school system. Everything was so new that Mercedez was failing. She did not have an interpreter because the school administrators explained they did not have special education. They told her mother that if she wanted an interpreter, she would have to pay for it out of her own pocket. As a result, her mom told her that if she wanted to go to a special school, they would move so she could attend one. However, Mother had just had a baby and Mercedez did not want to place that burden on her. Subsequently, she attended school without an interpreter or any assistive technology support.

Once school began, her classmates did not know her and were quite unkind in regard to her hearing issues. They were rude and mean, causing her to feel unusually insecure. She attempted to deny her hearing impairment. However, peers would cruelly remind her that she was different because she talked funny and kept asking them to repeat what they said. She felt alone during the whole year. Conversely, her teachers were very helpful and would work with her one-on-one as needed. Additionally, they would visit with her during breaks, keenly aware that her classmates were avoiding her. She was very thankful and states that they are the reason she settled in after a couple of months and completed eighth grade with As and Bs.

In ninth grade, Mercedez began high school. She describes her high school years as being full of drama. She was offered special education services but declined them because she knew that once she went into the real world she was not going to have somebody following her around to interpret what people said. Also, she believed the high school environment was a place to show people she was capable of learning on her own; she recognized that having a hearing impairment was not a downfall.

Moreover, her mother had introduced her to God and the Bible, which taught her to accept herself for who she was and to believe in herself. "Mother told me that God had made me deaf for a reason, and she encouraged me to not listen to the negative comments people were making." Her dad also predicted she would be very successful because being deaf had given her so much strength. Mercedez did believe she was strong because she recognized she had to work twice as hard as her classmates to understand the same material. She noticed that many of her classmates didn't seem to care about their education because they were not paying attention in class and were not doing their work. She was amazed that someone with perfect hearing could take it for granted.

Conversely, Mercedez was very focused. She did everything possible to ensure that she understood what was required of her, organizing her time and workload and completing her work daily. She was not embarrassed to raise her hand in class and ask questions, which in turn ensured that she understood the concepts taught and resulted in accurate, timely homework completion. She knew what she had to do, what she had to study for, and what her due dates were. Mercedez claims that being deaf forced her to be organized. She loved working hard, loved reading, loved getting information, and loved being educated. Her friends, on the other hand, were into music and boys and rarely studied.

In high school, some people from eighth grade had already spread the rumor that Mercedez was "deaf and dumb." Nevertheless, as students in the school got to know her, they became more accepting of her impairment. Sometimes they would go up to her and ask about her hearing aids, and she would show them because she was no longer ashamed. She appreciated being asked rather than being attacked and treated like someone who was stupid. Her new classmates gave her a chance to explain who she was. When they had that connection, "the students who had spread the rumors lost their power over me." The more people got to know her, the more they liked her. She had many friends.

Another rumor that was spread was that Mercedez was Muslim. Because of her looks and because America was in the post-9/11 era, the rumor was assumed to be true. This was very heartbreaking for Mercedez as it caused some people to treat her brutally. She tried to explain who she was, but many people chose to behave cruelly toward her. They would make comments such as, "Go back to where you came from." Sadly, she lost many friends.

Interestingly, Muslims on her campus asked her to join their group because they would see her alone. They would tell her they would protect her and she "did not have to worry about how the Americans were acting." They explained to her that they may not be the same blood, but they were her people. She developed a new circle of friends and, eight years later, is still friends with them. These friends are from various areas of the Middle East such as Pakistan and Afghanistan.

Mercedez's mother, who is from Iraq, is Christian; her father, who is also Christian, is from Mexico. She thinks it is strange that her "Christian" friends cast her aside believing she was Muslim, and it was her Muslim friends who were accepting of the fact she practices Christianity. She reasons that this experience has made her stronger; that is, she believes all people have the potential to be kind and ethical, and represent the best of mankind.

Mercedez wanted to join clubs in high school, but classmates who were already members made it clear she was not welcome because she was Muslim, or so they assumed. They gave her a difficult time, which scared her and made participation uncomfortable. She did not feel that she, as one person, could stand up to the group. In spite of this, she did attempt to participate in basketball, but without the ability to hear and with the echo and ambient noise in the gymnasium, she believed she would not be successful at that sport. She therefore decided to focus on her homework and schoolwork and "be with my kind."

Upon reflection, she wonders if having an interpreter present would have been helpful. She had chosen not to have one because she did not want people to feel sorry for her. She was keenly aware that her peers were judging her based on her appearance and felt dejected because this prevented them from objectively knowing who the person inside was.

Academically, Mercedez did well. She went to the school resource room only to take tests as she had the accommodation of extra testing time—ninety minutes. When she was finished, she would go to the special education secretary, who would give her a pass to her next class. All her teachers knew of her hearing impairment and accommodations, so they understood she would occasionally be late.

When Mercedez took the standardized state exam required by the No Child Left Behind (NCLB) Act, she went to the resource room because her interpreter was available. She had the same interpreter available to her all four years of high school, and this was helpful because it provided continuity. She found this person to be very helpful and is very grateful for her. She felt good about going to the resource room because she was able to get the clarification needed for anything she did not understand. She found it amusing that she took the same test as her general education friends but in a different environment. "Passing the state exam showed people that, although I have a hearing impairment, I am capable and intelligent; that is to say, they are separate issues—having an impairment or receiving special education services does not imply stupidity."

Mercedez began losing some of her already-limited hearing ability at age fifteen. She recalls speaking to her father on the phone and not being able to understand him, which she had been able to do in the past. She would have to ask him to repeat himself and speak louder. At the time, she thought she needed new hearing aids. After receiving them, she still had difficulty and could not distinguish words when they were articulated to her.

Her doctor told her she had lost a significant amount of hearing and explained she would continue to gradually lose her hearing until one day her world would be silent. The thought of never hearing her father's voice again "was the worst day of my life. I hated everyone in the world. But then my mom told me I needed to pray and God would give me a sign as to whether I should have a surgery or not."

Mercedez prayed, but she felt that God was taking too long to answer her. She briefly became very sad, but she did not stay that way for long. She decided she would live her life to the fullest. She plans on getting married one day, having kids, and enjoying everything just as she does today. Concerned that she might not be able to hear her kids call for her when they need her, her doctor responded, "That's what you have a husband for." This made her laugh and reassured her that everything is doable; the strategy she will have to use might look different from what she originally envisioned or from that of a hearing person, but that does not mean things cannot be done.

Curious about options, Mercedez asked her doctor about cochlear implants. Her doctor described the procedure to her and emphasized she had a 50 percent chance of the surgery's being successful. If it was not successful, the hearing she currently had would be gone forever. He stressed that the decision was hers. Mercedez had some friends who had had the surgery and didn't like it. One of the reasons is that they hear sounds they never heard before, such as someone tapping a pencil on the desk or the hum of lights. Because they have gone so many years without hearing these inconsequential background noises, they find it annoying and sometimes a bit painful.

Mercedez believed her friends should be thankful that they could hear these small noises and initially wanted the surgery; however, after finding her purpose (teaching English to others who are deaf) she decided she does not want to change who she is. "God made me this way for a reason and I want people to see that when I am a teacher I am like them, and this is why I am an excellent teacher." Therefore, she currently does not want the surgery. She speculates that she will always be able to read lips. Also, she understands that medical procedures improve and hopes that one day the odds will be greater that surgery may give her better hearing. For now, she is happy and credits her parents for giving her a good foundation that led to a great attitude.

Mercedez had annual individualized education program (IEP) meetings during which the participants discussed accommodations such as extra time and homework, using notes on tests, using calculators, receiving clarification, and others. She is grateful she had this support but wonders whether it was valuable in preparing her for the college environment. She notes that college is much harder than high school and the support she gets is much less extensive.

High school was very easy for her, lacking the challenge she needed to be better prepared for college. She had minimal class work and homework compared to her general education peers, and this resulted in her not being appropriately prepared for the workload she faces in the college environment. In high school she was given a lot of clarification if she did not understand what a question was asking. Conversely, at the college level, the teacher only reads the words as written and shrugs when asked for clarification, telling her, "Do your best." She currently does not get extra time for her tests because she does not ask for that accommodation even though she could.

Mercedez believes her IEP meetings were run well and addressed issues that were appropriate. For example, her teachers would share with her parents how well she was performing in class and would set proper annual goals such as coming to school early two days a week for extra help. There would also be some discussion about the most current medical interventions that might be appropriate for them to explore, such as the newest technology for hearing aids or surgery for cochlear implants. Teachers included her in their conversations. She states that teachers went the extra mile for her and she cannot think that anything could have been done better.

Mercedez remembers being asked about transition goals. She recalls dialogues about where she was going to live, what transportation she was going to use, what college she was going to attend, and options to determine her career path. Her team also discussed the need to get in touch with the disability service office, and some differences between the accommodations she would receive at the college level and those she received in high school. She admits that she did not fully understand these differences until she was actually in college and realized she had to do much more for herself. Thankfully, because she had learned fairly independently from the eighth grade through high school with no interpreter, she was well prepared to face her new challenges.

When Mercedez graduated from high school, she had not chosen a career. She went to her community college and took a test to determine what career fit her personality and abilities. At the top of the list was nursing, so she established that as her major. Mother was pleased. Father, on the other hand, expressed concerns about chemistry, biology, and similar subjects.

Initially, Mercedez believed that she would be OK in the more difficult nursing courses because for three years, from age seventeen to nineteen, she volunteered at the local hospital. She loved being around people and giving them comfort. She enjoyed sitting with patients after their surgery when no family was present. She would sit with them and listen to their stories and their lives and often leave crying because the experience was so emotional. She believed that if somebody needed help, you helped them. It made her very humble.

At one point she was in the elevator with a doctor who asked about her goals. She explained that she was about to graduate from high school and was going to go to college to be a nurse. He told her he would provide a letter of recommendation and see to it that her classes were paid for. She was very flattered and thankful. Later, she showed the doctor her curriculum and asked him if he thought she could successfully complete the course work. It was then that he realized she had a hearing impairment. He responded he was scared for her.

This doctor proceeded to "test" her hearing ability by saying two medical terms that were similar and asked her what the difference was. Mercedez could not aurally distinguish any difference and asked him what his point was. He said his point was she could have "a lot of death on her hands" because she might not hear spoken words correctly. This scared her because "I did not want anybody dying in my arms." Her mother told her she could do anything she wanted to and encouraged her to not listen to the doctor, but her father told her she might want to reconsider her educational goals. Confused, she did only her basic course work. When she was about to take biology, she realized her father was right—"nursing was not me."

At the end of her first year in the community college, more deaf students began to attend her school. Mercedez began to know and sign with them, which she had not done since seventh grade; she had to relearn how to sign. She shared her story with her friends and was embarrassed that she had been ashamed of her hearing impairment for so long. "It was a lesson regarding me being happy with who I am."

Mercedez has kept in touch with her hearing-impaired friends from high school via e-mail. She has found their communication skills very disconcerting because they often write as if they are still in the fourth grade. She is disappointed that their special education teachers permitted them to be complacent, resulting in a missed opportunity to gain linguistic fluency and content knowledge. She notes that she is successful and happy in college and speculates that this is because she did not allow herself to get comfortable in special education classes.

In retrospect, she is thankful that she stepped up to the challenge and was not scared to learn on her own. "I had already imagined college in my mind, and it is exactly as I thought it would be. I am very interested in school; I love all my classes, I feel normal but feel like I have become more sophisticated. It is one of the best feelings in the world when my teachers look at my work and are extremely impressed. They tell me I keep surprising them with good work."

Among her current group of hearing-impaired friends, she met a young man who was taking an English class. He knew only ASL and did not know different parts of the English language, for example, verbs, adjectives, and conjunctions. He asked Mercedez to tutor him and she realized he wrote just as he spoke ASL. Clearly, this is detrimental when writing at the college level. Mercedez was appalled to think this young man's teachers had not prepared him with college-level writing skills and wondered how he had gotten admitted.

She began to help him and worked with him for two hours. At the end he said to her, "Mercedez, you know how you are wondering what you want to do in your life? Remember how you said your mom said you were deaf for a reason? You know how you are a very hard worker and you can do anything you want to do? I really think you should be a deaf education teacher. You should teach English. You should teach hearing-impaired students how to read and write so we can be like you and not write at the third-grade level when we are in college."

That was the day when the lightbulb illuminated. "It was the best day of my life. I cried when he said that. It was as if God was speaking to me through him. I couldn't believe it."

Mercedez called her dad and told him, "I know what I want to do! I want to teach the hearing impaired how to read and write better." She then called her mom and said, "Mom, you were right. God did make me deaf for a reason!" Her mother responded in a celebratory voice, "I told you, I told you!" Mercedez exclaims, "It really was the best day ever!"

Mercedez talked to her adviser about what classes she needed to take for her new major. She understood it would take longer to get through school but believes the sacrifice is worth the payoff. She is frustrated, however, that the four-year school to which she will transfer keeps changing its requirements, making it more difficult for her to complete her prerequisites. Regardless, she remains hardworking, dedicated, and passionate.

She does admit feeling a bit impatient and eager to move forward, particularly in regard to working in a classroom with students she is sure she can help. She believes if it had not been for the young man she tutored, she would still be lost. She also realizes she had not believed what her mother had told her—that God had made her deaf for a reason. She now has a strong belief and faith in God because of all the things that have happened to her, things that have made her stronger.

Mercedez occasionally uses an interpreter for the classes that are most challenging for her. She wants to make sure she is on point with everything required. For math class, she does not use an interpreter because she is a visual learner and has difficulty dividing her attention between looking at the example on the board, reading the teacher's lips, and following the signing of her interpreter. She does use an interpreter for her education class because it is very active and group oriented. So many people may be discussing their ideas at once that she needs an interpreter to understand what the various students are saying. All her teachers know they need to look at her when they talk so she can read their lips, but she cannot see her classmates' lips when they talk.

Mercedez feels supported by her teachers and states that they have made it clear they want her to pass their classes. They frequently check in with her to ensure that she has understood the content discussed and knows what she needs to do for homework. Moreover, she feels successful because she took calculated baby steps when pursuing her postsecondary education. She takes four to five classes each semester because she wants to be a young, vibrant teacher who is active and able to provide a stimulating environment for her students. Also, she wants to be able to travel the world during her breaks and gain cultural enrichment.

Mercedez is involved in regular social activities at college, such as hanging out with friends. Her most frustrating moments occur when teachers show something to the class from YouTube with a voice talking in the background, with neither lips to read nor captioning, and she does not have an interpreter. She does her best to understand what is going on but feels left out. Otherwise, Mercedez says she likes college so much that if there were dorms on the campus, she would live in them so she could always be in the learning environment.

Regarding her hearing aids, Mercedez gets them adjusted every six months because her ears grow or because a part needs to be repaired. If something needs to be repaired on one of her hearing aids, she might go as long as two weeks without being able to hear in the ear without the aid. During this time, functioning within her world is more difficult. However, she accepts this as a small setback and remains optimistic. She was raised to see the positive side in both good and bad experiences and realizes that all experiences have helped her grow into a better person.

Mercedez says the best thing that has happened to her since she left high school is finding her purpose—studying to become an English teacher for the deaf. Additionally, she enjoyed being involved in the deaf club on campus. She was vice president for one semester and president for one year. During that time, she became more adept at signing and enjoyed teaching hearing people ASL. After a year and a half, she left the club, choosing to focus more on her classes.

Mercedez notes that several people have been instrumental in helping her attain success. Among them is the young man she tutored in English who opened up her eyes to seeking deaf education as a career. She also names the special education secretary, who was always helpful in regard to her needs to enter a class late because she had been testing. She had a teacher in high school who taught criminal justice with great passion. She says, "You could see the fire when she taught. She clearly cared about every student in her class."

She also names the teacher she had from prekindergarten through sixth grade who taught her how to read, write, and talk. She cherishes this teacher greatly and remains in contact with her to this day. "She was passionate, loved teaching deaf education, and is still the same." This teacher has encouraged her to complete her master's degree and then teach with her. She is excited about the prospect of teaming up with the former teacher who taught her everything because she is certain they could really make a difference in many lives, "a dream come true."

Mercedez's advice to other students with hearing impairments is to not let others tell them they can't do something. She encourages others to embrace who they are and to remember that God made them and he does not make mistakes. "Maybe you don't understand 'why' now, but one day you will have a 'lightbulb moment,' and it will be the happiest moment of your life. Even though things may get hard and you make it to a point where you feel there is no purpose, choose to keep going. It is often after struggling that you experience an accomplishment that shows you anything is possible if you put your mind to it. Remember that technology keeps evolving, which leads to hope that hearing aids will be smaller and surgeries will be more successful, helping the hearing impaired to hear like normal people. Have faith and keep moving forward."

Mercedez's advice to teachers is to be patient when working with hearing-impaired students. Don't give up if you need to repeat yourself more than three times; hearing impaired students often view their teachers as their only ally when attempting to successfully navigate the hearing world. "Teach us to be fearless and to read more. That is what helps us conquer the world. Teach from the heart and remember we all live under the same sky; we just have a different light in our lives. Be that light so we can see. Remember, our eyes are our ears. Go the extra mile and God will reward you."

Mercedez feels very blessed to know both ASL and English. She hopes to use her gift to create a better future for others with a hearing impairment. Recognizing that students with a label often remain in special education and are frequently treated differently from their peers, she wants to enlighten them; the possibilities are many if they are willing to work to obtain their dreams. "They should believe the sky is the limit; they can be and do anything they want to be and do. There is beauty in connecting, networking, and socializing. Being deaf is not a downfall."

She also wants to educate teachers about those with a hearing impairment, mainly imparting the fact that "deaf people are not stupid. Given appropriate instruction and time, they can learn. Not hearing sounds or voices does not mean they cannot communicate." She wants to be inspiring and encouraging, settling for no excuses. "My students will be very lucky to have me, and I am very lucky to have realized my purpose in living on God's green earth."

TIPS FOR TEACHERS OF STUDENTS WITH HEARING IMPAIRMENT

- Prior to instruction, establish expectations for turn taking and engagement, for example, students will look at the speaker.
- Provide concrete activities.
- Preteach, reviewing key terms and concepts to be learned.
- Identify specific questions the students should consider when reading.
- Find interesting reading material and have informal discussions that focus on the ideas and information.
- Link prior experiences with the reading content.
- Think aloud when inferring meaning from pictures, key words, graphics and texts.
- Inform the student how to determine if inferences are correct.
- Model the "think aloud" process.
- Scaffold increasingly sophisticated reasoning strategies.
- Emphasize skills such as comparing, sequencing, and identifying patterns.
- Provide direct instruction for sight words, root words, prefixes, suffixes, morphemes, phonics, fluency, expository, and narrative reading strategies.
- Use graphic organizers to show how key concepts are related.
- Blog about the study topic and have students engage in a group discussion.
- Include virtual experiences, such as viewing captioned educational media, then conduct group discussions about the topic.
- End lessons with summarizing, problem solving, and linking learning to living via performance-based assessments.
- Permit students to use notes to identify and summarize lesson content.
- Face the students when speaking.
- Reduce background noise.
- Establish routine attention-getting strategies, for example, flickering the lights.
- Provide sufficient wait time.
- Use technology such as overhead projectors and Smart Boards.
- Post a schedule for visual reference.
- Do not assume an interpreter is a tutor.
- Provide textbooks to interpreters so they can become familiar with the material being taught.

- It is permissible for interpreters to request clarification of spoken messages.

TIPS FOR STUDENTS WITH HEARING IMPAIRMENT

- Practice RAP: <u>R</u>ead the paragraph, <u>A</u>sk oneself the main idea, <u>P</u>ut the main idea in one's own words.
- Implement the PARS strategy: <u>P</u>review by scanning headings and chapter summaries, <u>A</u>sk and record questions about the main ideas gleaned from scanning, <u>R</u>ead the chapters, <u>S</u>ummarize the main ideas that answer the recorded questions.
- Consistently use assistive technology.
- Ask for a note taker, sign language interpreter, or tutor as needed.
- Create graphic organizers to connect ideas and concepts.

REFERENCE

Luckner, J. L., Slike, S. B., & Johnson, H. (2012, March/April). Helping students who are deaf or hard of hearing succeed. *Teaching Exceptional Children, 44*(4), 58–67.

Chapter 9

Mercedez's Mother's Story

Hearing Impairment

Mercedez was the first child and grandchild born into her mother's family, so she received a lot of attention and affection from everyone. As a toddler, although she did not speak as many words as others her age, she would say simple words such as "mom" and "dad" in Aramaic, Spanish, and English. Without any siblings to compare her to, Mother thought her minimal speech was due to an innate desire to remain quiet. She knew children learn to talk at different rates, so she initially did not find Mercedez's lack of speech particularly alarming. However, as Mercedez got older and was clearly lagging farther and farther behind others her age, Mother had her evaluated by a doctor. After conducting the evaluation, the doctor did not think there was a problem.

One day Mercedez was playing in the front yard and a car was coming down the street. Wanting to ensure she was safe, Mother called for her to come but Mercedez did not respond to her. As Mother got closer, Mercedez eventually heard or saw her and cheerfully said, "Hello, Mom!" Reflecting back, Mother wonders if she was in denial that there was a problem.

Mother also wonders if, because Mercedez was the first child of the family, she was not as cognizant of the issue because she had no other child against whom to measure Mercedez's progress. At that time, she thought her daughter was behaving the way she was because she was spoiled; Mother believed her unresponsiveness would improve with time. Looking back, she now recognizes that Mercedez's unresponsiveness in various situations was because there was indeed a problem with her ability to hear.

Mother states that it was Mercedez's father who first recognized that Mercedez did not hear. He insisted they take her to the doctor, who explained that Mercedez's eardrum was almost nonexistent, so sounds were not being vibrated to the inner ear. Additionally, she had very few hairs in her inner ear, greatly reducing her hearing capacity. She received her first hearing aids at age four. She began speech therapy and learned how to read lips and use sign language when she entered the public school system.

When Mercedez began school, the speech-language pathologist evaluated Mercedez and presented the results in layman's terms. Still, Mother did not want to hear what the speech-language pathologist was telling her because the information was heartbreaking. She did not understand why Mercedez had been born deaf because nobody in her family had dealt with this issue prior to this moment. She frequently cried because she loved her daughter and did not want her to have a difficult life. Mother states that she turned everything over to the Lord, believing that there was a reason he had created Mercedez with a hearing impairment. Mother has a very strong faith and chose to be thankful for her daughter rather than resentful of the impending struggles she was sure to face.

While in school, Mercedez was separated from her general education peers in the morning and placed in the special education resource environment. This environment consisted of students with various exceptionalities. Mercedez would tell her mother that she did not like being there. She wanted to be with the other students because that was where she felt comfortable. That is to say, she wanted to learn like everybody else and attend general education classes all day, not just in the afternoon.

However, her morning classes were important because her teachers pre-taught what she would have to learn in her afternoon classes. They also taught her how to speak, lipread, and sign, which was and continues to be beneficial for her. Yet she felt embarrassed when she was segregated from her friends. When Mercedez would come home from school and complain that she could not understand her teachers, Mother would sympathize with her. Not knowing what else to do, she prayed that the Lord would be with her.

Mother believed that something miraculous was going to happen and Mercedez would acquire the ability to hear. She still believes this as technology continually improves. Mercedez periodically has to go to the doctor to receive new hearing aids because she outgrows them or because one breaks or malfunctions. It was explained that when she was finished growing, there was a possibility that she could have surgery to improve her hearing ability. When Mercedez turned eighteen, she and her mother talked to her doctor about the possibilities of surgery. It was explained that if surgery were conducted and not successful, the little bit of hearing she currently had would be lost forever.

Mercedez did not want to take the risk of losing any hearing and opted to keep her hearing aids. Everybody agreed with her decision. They loved Mercedez for who she was, they were going to accept the fact that she was deaf, and they were thankful to God for her. So, while Mother still holds the hope that one day there will be a remarkable surgery that will permit Mercedez to hear sounds clearly, she loves Mercedez exactly the way God made her.

Mother states there was a long period of time in which Mercedez was not comfortable with being deaf. For example, she would hide her hearing aids by wearing her hair down to cover them. The fact that Mercedez was embarrassed to show her ears distressed her mother, but she never insisted she behave in a way that was uncomfortable or embarrassing for her. She understood that Mercedez's impairment was something Mercedez would have to come to terms with in her own time, so she helped her daughter learn how to accept herself. In the end, Mother just wanted Mercedez to be happy with what God had given her and be grateful for how he had made her.

Mother asserts that we must always say, "Thank you, Lord" and not complain. She further says that we live in a beautiful country and we have everything we really need to live comfortably, leaving us no room to grumble. Ultimately, as she grew older, Mercedez began to wear her hair up, which signified to Mother that she had developed acceptance of who she was. Mother was pleased that Mercedez understood that one's physical appearance is not who he or she is emotionally and spiritually.

Prior to living with Mother, Mercedez lived with her father in Texas through the seventh grade. She came to live with her mother when she turned thirteen. At that point Mercedez was speaking well but had minimal hearing. The school she attended planned to provide an interpreter for her, but she declined to accept the help from the eighth grade through high school. Her teachers knew she was deaf, so they placed her in the front of the classroom so she could read their lips. "All of her teachers were very willing to help her. I told Mercedez that God was quick to take care of her and was doing so by providing the necessary people to help her."

Mother attended the annual individualized education program (IEP) meetings and believes she was appropriately included. She describes the teams as "very nice people who explained issues and strategies to me in terms I could understand." She avers that everybody in Mercedez's life has been nice and helpful, encouraging Mercedez to succeed. The team listened to Mercedez's wishes and agreed that if she wanted to be in regular education classes, then that was where she should be.

Mother believes that the classes Mercedez took prepared her appropriately for college. She notes that many of the teachers would take time after school, going the extra mile by working one-on-one with her. Everyone was keenly aware of Mercedez's determination and hard work. In spite of the extra help she received, Mercedez was frequently frustrated that she could not hear her teachers. She feared she was missing crucial information and would consequently fail her classes. "She was very conscientious and eager to do well."

High school was rough for Mercedez because she tried to hide her hearing impairment. The environment was full of teenage drama and Mercedez was embarrassed to tell people she could not hear them. Mother suggests that people with hearing impairments discuss their exceptionality with others because it will help the others understand their unique issues and shed light on the reason they are not responding when spoken to. "Everyone should be proud of who they are."

During her high school years, Mercedez was involved in a few fights because others would bully her. The administrators knew the altercations occurred because Mercedez had been taunted. Mercedez was suspended along with the others involved; Mother agreed with this decision because everyone was equally accountable and needed to learn that fighting was not the way to solve disputes. Mercedez needed to learn that being "cool" meant being popular in the correct group. Mother was strict with her because she wanted Mercedez to learn how to respect herself. She would often pray with her about this matter.

Mercedez told her mother that people would make comments that she had an accent. Upon hearing this, Mother would encourage her to talk to her peers about her hearing impairment because educating them about her issue would result in understanding. Mercedez also told her mother that the girls in school thought she was stuck up because she would not respond to them when they would say hello to her. Again, Mother encouraged her to share her story so that they would understand her condition. "I wanted Mercedez to be grateful for who she was."

Eventually, at the end of high school, Mercedez mustered up the courage to explain that she was deaf. Mother felt proud of her for gathering her nerve. Mother reiterated that "God has a plan for us which is much better than our own plan. We should always be thankful."

Mercedez would relocate to a different classroom when testing so that an interpreter would be available to her if she needed a question clarified. Mother felt this was very helpful. "When she is in a regular classroom there are often muffled noises which distract her. Providing a quiet place in which she could think was appropriate."

Mercedez was always prepared because she was always eager to learn. "Mercedez's struggles are no different than those who can hear. Some subjects are easier than others to learn; we all struggle with certain concepts. While the lack of hearing may cause her to have to focus harder, it has ultimately made her a stronger person."

When Mercedez was going to graduate from high school, Mother knew that college was the next step. The IEP team did well discussing her transition needs. She thought Mercedez was going to become a nurse, but a discussion with a doctor clarified the challenges she would face that could carry serious consequences affecting the lives of her patients. Over time, the conversation evolved to the possibility of becoming a teacher of hearing-impaired students.

"She has a big heart and wants to work with children. Many fields require a big heart; choosing a career for money is a wrong choice. One should choose a career because they believe they have something to offer and they are willing to work hard to attain the necessary skills to enrich those around them. Some people who are in the 'helping fields' such as education, medicine, social work, clergy, counselors, occupational therapists, and speech-language pathologists should not be there because they do not have the heart; they are just going through the motions. Don't work for the money or tenure, work for the love."

Mercedez was very excited when she chose a career in education. She wants to be the teacher in her students' lives who makes a difference, just like certain teachers she has had in her life. "Mercedez is a natural helper with a good heart who has patience. Teachers are like a student's mother and have much to offer because they impart moral values as well as academic knowledge."

Mother can easily see her daughter being happy in the teaching profession and believes she can make a real difference. Without such teachers, student growth is stunted. Mother also believes this is one reason God made her daughter deaf: so she can reach out to others like her. "Knowing sign language is akin to knowing another language. Teaching American Sign Language (ASL) and teaching others how to lipread will help her students rise to new heights. Also, teaching them how to write the way hearing people do will provide more opportunities for them."

When Mercedez began attending college, she was having problems hearing her professors, so the disability service office personnel offered an interpreter for her. She used the interpreters only a few times but told her mother she felt more confused when they were present because she had to divide her attention between looking at the interpreter and attempting to read the teachers' lips. She kept insisting that she could successfully complete her classes without any assistance. Mother supported her decision and the interpreter stopped attending class with her. The result was that Mercedez struggled to understand course content because she could not always see her teachers' lips when they were writing on the board. Mother explained to her that the help offered by college personnel was for her so that she could benefit; it was not for anyone else. Mercedez agreed to accept the assistance of the interpreters on an as-needed basis.

Mother recalls a college teacher Mercedez had who was very cold to Mercedez. When she would ask him a question, he would respond harshly. For example, when answering a question on a test, she wanted to be sure she understood it correctly. She asked the teacher if she was writing the answer in a manner that was acceptable. His response was that if she had read the question then she would know if she was getting it right. When Mercedez would clarify that she simply wanted to know if in his opinion she understood the question correctly, he would respond that if she had to question herself then maybe her answer was not right.

Mercedez found this professor's response to be patronizing and unhelpful, but Mother explained to her that God puts in our lives people who help us learn even when we don't immediately recognize the lesson. She told Mercedez, "People are put in our paths that are going to help prepare us for future needs. People are not always going to be accommodating."

After finals, this "harsh" professor asked to speak with Mercedez in the hallway. He asked her how she felt about the finals and if she thought she had passed. She responded that it was challenging but she felt she had passed with a B. He mentioned how he had been harsh with her that semester. Mercedez responded that he was mean, had not helped her, and that she felt he did not like her.

The professor responded that in the real world nobody was going to hold her hand or pat her back or feel sorry for her. He said, "So you think you have passed my class with a B, correct?" Mercedez said she did and the professor responded, "You are the one who passed—on your own without being coddled." This made sense to her; she earned her grade because she did the required work—nothing was handed to her. She realized that this was the professor's way of preparing her for what she was going to have to face in the real world.

Still, Mercedez found this teacher to be scary because she had never had an instructor who was so harsh. He explained to her that she would understand more completely why he used his approach when she became a teacher. She was taken aback when he reiterated that he had not done anything extra to help her, just as she would not do anything extra to help her future students. Mercedez does believe that she is going to go the extra mile because she recognizes the impact the extra effort can have. She suggests that this instructor was thinking about his time investment and was comparing it to his paycheck. Spending additional time to assist her would result in a reduced return on investment.

Conversely, she views her career as one in which she will be helping others. She believes the money she receives along the way is going to be a gift from God and that he will see to all her needs such as paying her bills, buying food, and keeping a roof over her head. Mother used this opportunity as a lesson for Mercedez, saying this professor was an example of the kind of teacher she did not want to be and that learning these kinds of lessons is just as important as learning lessons from those you want to emulate. Mother encouraged Mercedez to attend class and learn the best she could and not lower herself to this instructor's level.

Mother states that the best thing that has happened to Mercedez academically since graduating from high school has been going to college and learning from both her positive and negative experiences. "When one goes through life, all of their experiences make them who they are. Knowing Mercedez is experiencing life like any other person is rewarding. Finishing her associates degree and entering a four-year college is an enormous accomplishment for someone with a hearing impairment." She believes the most instrumental people in Mercedez's life who have had a positive impact on her are her dad because he is her strength, herself because she is her confidant and has a strong faith, her grandparents because they love and support her, and the teacher she had in Texas who taught her how to sign and read lips. Mother wants Mercedez to be like that teacher because she was such a great role model.

Mother notes that she never pushed Mercedez because she never wanted her to be frustrated. She prayed for her and placed Mercedez at Jesus's feet, trusting that He would take care of her needs. The result is that "she has always been a good student and a great daughter. She works hard in spite of the difficulties she faces. She is always warm, always well behaved, a hard worker, internally inspired, and strong."

Mother's advice to other parents with a hearing-impaired child is to have faith. God walked with her and dried the tears she had for her daughter. He helped her learn that being deaf was not a bad thing.

"Do not treat your hearing-impaired child any differently than you treat your hearing children. Understand having an exceptional child is a gift from God. Ultimately, you are going to learn more from them than they learn from you. God gives us our children to take care of them. Stay in your faith and the correct people will be brought in to help you. You do not have to be brilliant to help your child be successful. Be thankful for all things and love your kids—your love will make them strong."

TIPS FOR PARENTS OF STUDENTS WITH HEARING IMPAIRMENT

- Get your child's hearing evaluated as soon as you suspect there is a problem.
- Seek interventions as soon as possible—the sooner assistance is received, the better the chance of the child's reaching his or her potential.

- Provide the same love and discipline as you give to any child.
- Allow natural consequences to occur—that is how one learns and grows.
- Remember that the lack of hearing does not mean an inability to be successful.
- Maintain a positive attitude.
- Seek resources to help you learn how to be actively involved in your child's education and extracurricular activities.
- Peruse the Internet for local organizations or enter online chat rooms.
- If your child is an infant, interact by holding, facing, smiling, and responding to him or her.
- If your child is older, post charts to help him or her understand what he or she needs to do.
- Talk to your child in a natural way.
- Label items to help your child learn them.
- Discuss medical devices and other options with your child and his or her doctor.
- Participate in community programs developed for hearing-impaired children.
- Contact your public school immediately so your child can begin to receive services through the Child Find early intervention programs (up to entry into kindergarten).
- If your child is of school age, work with your child's school to ensure that he or she is receiving the appropriate support such as extra time to complete tests, opportunities to test in quiet areas, interpreters, or assistive technology.
- Learn techniques used by your child's teacher(s) and imitate them at home.
- Help your child become independent and self-sufficient.
- Encourage your child to socialize.
- Be involved in your child's life—research shows this strategy results in higher positive outcomes.
- Balance the demands on your time with fun—stay in touch with your friends, engage in enjoyable activities, and have a date night with your spouse.

REFERENCES

Adnani, S. (2009, May 19). Parent's role in teaching hearing impaired children. BrightHub. Retrieved from http://www.brighthub.com/education/special/articles/35493.aspx.

Goss, H. V. (2010, May 9). Tips for parents of hearing impaired children. Livestrong. Retrieved from http://www.livestrong.com/article/119480-tips-parents-hearing-impaired-children/.

Isaacson, B. (2010, August 16). Hope for parents of children with hearing loss. WebMD. Retrieved from http://www.webmd.com/parenting/help-for-parents-hearing-impaired-children.

Chapter 10

Mike's Story

Learning Exceptionality in Reading and Mathematics

When Mike was six years old, his teachers recognized that he did not understand reading and math concepts as well as his classmates did. Fortunately, his perceptive teachers immediately called his mother and shared their observations. Mother was already cognizant of this issue but was unsure how to move forward. As a result of their conversation, Mike's teachers placed him in a pullout resource support room while Mother found some fun books and diligently read with him for about twenty minutes every night. As a result of Mother's timely early intervention, Mike acquired a joy of reading that might have otherwise eluded him. Enhancing his reading skills at an early age allowed him to overcome his reading difficulties and prevented him from requiring assistance in this subject after third grade. "By the time I entered high school, I was reading at the college level."

Mike never had an issue with writing. Math was another matter. Mike struggled with understanding basic operations and could not seem to grasp rudimentary concepts that required minimal analysis. Thus, in elementary school, Mike was required to physically get up and walk out of his general education classroom to attend resource math class.

He felt this visual movement was embarrassing and made him feel "dumb." When friends asked him why he was leaving and where he was going, he would be at a loss for words and would say nothing. Leaving his general education math class was so upsetting he would shut down. Subsequently, he was not open to receiving the help his resource teachers were attempting to provide for him because he was already mad about being required to learn math in a classroom away from his friends. He suggests an alternative strategy might be for all students to take math the first period of the day. That way, the absence of students with exceptionalities would not be obvious and the embarrassment would be ameliorated.

Overall, Mike does not believe the pullout program was helpful because all fifteen to twenty resource students were taught the same information in the same manner by the same teacher, and no special assistance was given to individuals. An exception to this occurred in one grade in which students were divided into different groups based on concepts that needed remediation. In this instance, the resource teacher helped Mike by focusing on his specific need as opposed to teaching around it or missing it altogether because too many students' needs were being addressed at one time. For example, if Mike did not understand how to tell time, he was placed in a group with other students who did not know how to tell time. By targeting the specific area of deficiency, the teacher helped Mike learn more effectively.

Another strategy that helped Mike was being permitted to work on one concept at a time on a whiteboard at his desk or at the board on the classroom wall. First, his teacher would assist him by providing step-by-step instructions as he painstakingly worked through the imposing problem. Next, his teacher would let him use the first problem as a visual aid and then she would provide verbal prompts as needed as he slowly worked through the next couple of problems. Eventually, Mike would no longer need verbal prompts.

In the evening when Mike would attempt to complete his homework, so much would have happened between his math class and homework time that he would once again be overwhelmed with having to recall so much information. Gradually, he learned to implement the strategies the teacher used with him on the board. He would refer back to similar problems he had completed in class and apply those steps to his homework problems. This took an immense amount of effort and created continuous frustration. Mike believes that if he had been permitted to complete fewer problems than his general education peers, he might have been more open to learning the myriad of math concepts that he encountered. Instead, facing problems on both sides of his worksheet plunged him into a state of frustration and made him feel as if this whole business of solving math problems was an exercise in futility.

The requirement to attend a separate math class changed at the junior high level. In this new school, students rotated for all classes. So, when it came time for Mike to attend math class, he rotated into that class while all the students were rotating into their next class. He therefore felt an immense amount of relief because he was not sticking out like a sore thumb by being the "obvious" student who needed help.

Mike recalls one math teacher at the junior high level who would tell him to finish what he could. She would look at the completed problems to see if he understood the concept involved. Mike found this to be very helpful because he wasn't facing an insurmountable number of problems to solve and he was given credit and praise for what he knew, as opposed to having points deducted for incomplete work. Still, Mike struggled with the abstract concepts involved in math, was extremely overwhelmed, and experienced multiple "shutdowns" due to his frustrations. An additional issue during this time was the rebellious peers in his resource class who were constantly interfering with the teacher's instruction time. These students required the teacher's attention and prevented Mike from being taught a large amount of significant material.

Mike's struggles in math did not affect his ability to make friends. He recalls carrying himself with a great air of confidence. He is friendly, gregarious, and nonjudgmental, and he has a laid-back personality. Thus, he had many friends in the lunchroom, at recess, and during extracurricular activities. He did, however, make every attempt to avoid classmates who were working on math problems during recess and breaks.

In these awkward situations, usually one unprepared classmate was copying the completed work of another, proficient classmate. If Mike happened to step into this uncomfortable situation, his classmates would ask him if he had completed his homework. Because he was not in the same math class, he did not have the same work and would therefore feel embarrassed that the question was even posed to him. He was concerned he would be placed in the same humiliating category as other students who were made fun of because they appeared "dumb." In retrospect, Mike recognizes that this was a self-imposed perception although at the time it felt very real.

Mike eventually entered high school not knowing his times tables. This was discovered by another teacher he knew—not his math teacher. This teacher contacted the school's resource math teacher who worked with students at the same ability level as Mike. This resource math teacher was able to assist Mike directly because she had a couple of aides in her room who could work with the other students while she focused on Mike's needs. Mike's preference to receive one-on-one instruction and his desire to learn coupled with his teacher's ability to provide proper instruction helped him quickly understand concepts with which he had previously struggled.

For example, this teacher used manipulatives so he could visually and tangibly divide fifteen tiles into three groups of five to demonstrate $3 \times 5 = 15$. This teacher would consistently teach the same concept (i.e. multiplication) until she knew the student had mastered it. Required to keep a notebook, Mike suddenly realized that he was making a lot of progress quickly. This provided visual affirmation that he was capable, and it inspired him to work harder. Mike was so focused and his teacher was so organized and proficient with her instruction that in approximately two months he understood almost all the basic concepts and was able to enter the resource class for algebra at the ninth-grade level.

Mike does not recall ever attending an individualized education program (IEP) meeting during elementary and junior high school. He does not remember anyone's meeting with him and his mother to discuss his needs, to discuss what he could and could not do, or to set goals for the coming year. He believes the only time he was included in a meeting was in high school, but he does not specifically recollect sitting with his teachers and parent to discuss his progress or his needs. The only explanation for his exceptionality that Mike recalls receiving was that it was not a bad thing, that he just needed extra help. No one explained to him that his intelligence fell within the normal range and that he was not "dumb." In fact, it was his high school algebra teacher who took the time to explain to him what a learning disability in math meant and expounded on his positive attributes and competencies.

At a young age, Mike recognized that other students struggled with various academic subjects. He therefore did not understand why he was singled out as requiring additional help when his struggling classmates were permitted to stay in the same room. One day in high school, he was enlightened when his algebra teacher shared various stories regarding her struggles. He felt more "normal" because if a "smart teacher" struggled with certain concepts, it made sense that he might struggle also. He continued to work very hard but found the new concepts he was learning difficult to retain. He understood that one concept built on another, but he struggled to apply what he already knew to when he was trying to learn. He almost always eventually understood the new concept, but this was accomplished after expending a great amount of effort —far beyond what his peers had to do to be successful.

Mike's goal after high school was to join the military. Because no IEP meeting was ever held with Mike present, no one within the special education department ever discussed this transition goal with him. Mike's high school district had a transition specialist who was supposed to meet with every student with an exceptionality, teach them all how to complete an application, instruct them on how to write a résumé, describe how one should dress when approaching a potential employer, and practice the interview process. Additionally, Mike was supposed to receive a list of potential community-based organizations that could help him attain his postsecondary goals. This never occurred. He says that the first time he received instructions regarding how to complete a résumé was when he left the military.

Mike feels lucky despite not meeting with the transition specialist because he was involved in the Junior Reserve Officers' Training Corps (JROTC). He had an instructor who gave him many helpful hints about how to prepare for the Armed Services Vocational Aptitude Battery (ASVAB), the military admissions test; what he could expect when training in boot camp; and what career options the various military branches offered. Mike initiated contact with his military recruiter and completed all the required steps to meet his goal.

Mike states that the best time of his school day was history class. He liked learning about different wars, what events caused them, what happened during them, and battle strategies that were implemented. He also liked government and believes these classes were instrumental in preparing him to become a more knowledgeable member of the military. He also believes his English classes were enjoyable and helpful; he has had to write many reports in his postsecondary careers and is proficient because of the skills he learned.

Mike believes the tests he took in elementary school were reasonable and covered information that had been taught in class. Depending on the purpose of the test, sometimes he was permitted to use a calculator and sometimes he was not. He thinks there was a suitable amount of questions for the time allotted, and the problems posed were appropriate—some being easier and some being more challenging. He thinks teaching information and testing concepts learned is most meaningful when it is perceived as relevant by the student. He believes teaching information just because it exists in the textbook does not necessarily make it meaningful. He understands that students don't necessarily know what information they are going to need in their unknown future career, but he believes some concepts can be saved for more specialized courses such as calculus or trigonometry.

Regarding the state standardized test, Mike thinks it tested too much information for a student with an exceptionality to complete in one sitting. He reflects that one should not be tested at once on every concept he or she has ever learned; rather, testing students at various intervals is more reasonable. Acceptable parameters should be predetermined and occur in increments. "Just because someone cannot remember everything that was ever taught to them does not mean that person cannot be successful in the real world. Not every math concept is relevant to one individual student."

Mike states that one of the best strategies elementary teachers used was not treating him differently from his friends just because he struggled with math. He also believes that the fact they were not easier on him in spite of his mathematical struggles was helpful in the long run (although it didn't feel like it at the time!). The greatest obstacle he had to overcome was coping with the overwhelming amount of math that was thrown at him. As soon as he got overwhelmed, he could not focus on anything. He was not trying to be stubborn; he simply could not even think about how to start the problem. This feeling of inadequacy sometimes carried over into the next day; it was as if a wall had been erected and it was too high to scale.

Mike believes that there needs to be balance between being too easy on a student and not giving work too far beyond the student's ability. Students with exceptionalities know that it usually takes longer to complete their assignments, so their anxiety level often automatically elevates. Mike never wanted somebody to be too easy on him; he knew that had no value. However, receiving too much information at once was overwhelming and crippling.

He suggests that a reasonable strategy is to relate math problems to real-life situations. This makes math much more meaningful to the learner. Also, when teachers are not afraid to show their weaknesses and discuss their struggles, it makes the teacher appear more approachable.

Mike says that the best thing that has helped him since high school is attending community college. He has taken some college math classes and implements strategies he learned in junior high and high school. For example, he will work on a whiteboard to clarify the necessary steps he needs to understand to solve the particular type of problem on which he is working. Also, he has a patient, built-in tutor in his home: his wife.

Although he does not have an associates degree, Mike currently has forty credit hours, earning straight As with the exception of two Bs in his classes. This is an accomplishment of which he is immensely proud. He had a eureka moment when he realized he could successfully solve college-level math problems even though it takes him longer than some of his peers. He is successful in the college environment and enjoys learning with his peers. For those who struggle with any subject, he states, "If you can get over your embarrassment, you can ask for help and receive it—swallow your pride."

After graduating from high school, Mike went into the military at the age of eighteen, joining the security forces that guarded strategic assets for the government. He later went into the infantry. Both of these experiences helped him in his current career in the police force. After he was honorably discharged from the military, he enrolled in community college, taking some criminal justice classes. He feels confident when giving a presentation and says that everything he learned in both the military and in his criminal justice classes has helped in his current career as a police officer.

Mike competed against more than eight hundred people for the three positions that were available within his local police force. He had to pass an intense multi-subject test, undergo an interview process, and pass a physical fitness test to be selected for the police academy. He felt intimidated but promised himself he would give his best effort. The result was that he received higher scores than those who had obtained their bachelors and masters degrees, was admitted to the police academy, and demonstrated the mental and physical toughness required to graduate from the program. He is proud that he has overcome many obstacles as a person with an exceptionality and is a contributing citizen to his community. He believes that his success is the culmination of his JROTC experience; his English, government, and history classes; and his military experience.

The most disappointing thing that has happened since Mike left high school is the appearance of factors that have made it difficult to remain in college. As a new police officer working shifts, he has a one-year probation period and is required to work overtime as required. He worries that time away from the educational environment will cause him to lose the mind-set required to study. He knows many officers who choose to work overtime rather than return to school because overtime pay is lucrative in the short run—working to pay the bills while attending school is very challenging. Mike remains determined to obtain his bachelor's degree one day in spite of the plethora of obstacles he will have to overcome.

Mike's advice to others with learning exceptionalities like him:

- Do not let the embarrassment hold you up.
- Permit other people, programs, or resources to help you.
- Use Purplemath.com as a helpful online resource.
- Commit time to your education with no excuses.
- Work on your specific issue by dedicating ten to thirty minutes to it every night.
- Keep a notebook of what you have completed so you can see your progress.
- Build a relationship with the person or people who help you.
- Don't get down on yourself.
- Don't let your frustration stand in the way of your goal.

Mike wishes someone had sat with him one-on-one much earlier (like his high school math teacher did). He believes he would have been much more successful much earlier if the strategies he learned had been taught to him earlier. As for parents, he believes involvement in their child's education immensely improves the chances of success. "Being willing to admit your child has a need and immediately addressing it is the optimal approach."

TIPS FOR TEACHERS OF STUDENTS WITH MATH EXCEPTIONALITIES

- Prioritize instruction around critical content.
- Preteach requisite skills before introducing new material.
- Allow use of a calculator while emphasizing the math process.
- Model sequences of steps, provide demonstrations, and use hands-on learning with manipulatives.
- Color-code operations or steps.
- Scaffold instruction: I do it, we do it, you do it.
- Create a reference sheet.
- Seat the student with a knowledgeable peer tutor.
- Use a whiteboard.
- Verbally explain steps at first, then progressively remove verbal explanations until the student no longer needs them.

- Use clear, concise language.
- Provide sample problems for reference.
- Ensure that all math operations and symbols are recognized and understood.
- Confirm mastery of one skill before introducing the next.
- Teach to all learning modalities (visual, auditory, and kinesthetic).
- Provide frequent, meaningful review opportunities.
- Create opportunities for active learning as opposed to passive memorization.
- Reduce the number of problems to be completed.
- Give alternative assignments as necessary.
- Deliver timely feedback.
- Collaborate with fellow faculty members regarding content to ensure that standards are consistently implemented.
- Use mnemonics, for example, PEMDAS (Please Excuse My Dear Aunt Sally) for the order of operations.
- Teach with board games, cards, and dice.

TIPS FOR PARENTS OF STUDENTS WITH MATH EXCEPTIONALITIES

- Ensure that an individualized education program (IEP) is in place.
- Reduce distractions by turning off the radio and TV.
- Complete work in the same study area every day.
- Tutor your child and provide samples as appropriate.
- Write a contract delineating when homework is to be completed.
- Read the directions with your child to be sure they are understood.
- Practice the addition and times tables as appropriate.
- Break homework into smaller time segments if your child experiences frustration, for example, allow the child to work for fifteen minutes and take a ten-minute break.
- Praise your child.
- Complete problems that have similar operations at the same time, for example, solve all addition problems, then subtraction problems, then multiplication problems, and so forth.
- Organize work in a notebook.
- Develop a chart and check off items as they are completed to show progress.
- Hire a tutor if you are unable to assist your child.
- Be consistent.
- Communicate with the teacher on a regular basis.

- Check the finished product.
- Provide occasional rewards for good effort and completed work.

TIPS FOR STUDENTS WITH MATH EXCEPTIONALITIES

- Avoid working in front of the television or in other areas that provide distractions.
- Accept your disability—it does not mean you are dumb or lazy.
- Attempt to become informed about your brain's functioning and its processing difficulties.
- Ask the school psychologist about strategies you might use that make sense to you.
- Common accommodations include extra time, outlines, hands-on activities, borrowed notes, and shortened assignments.
- When discussing accommodations, speak up about what works for you and what does not.
- You might have an idea about how you can do better even if it is not formally recorded; share that idea with your teachers.
- Talk to your teachers about your needs as soon as possible; for example, what teaching style helps you, what distracts you, what kinds of assignments work best for you, and what helps clear up concepts for you.
- Know your rights so you can articulate your needs, but refrain from taking advantage of these rights by asking for accommodation you do not need.
- Know your strengths—you may learn better by seeing a problem solved, by hearing the steps to solve it, or by manipulating objects to help you understand how to solve it.
- Be willing to compromise on what the teacher can provide for you within the confines of the environment.
- Use a highlighter.
- Test in a quiet area if that helps.
- Take your time and ask for clarification if you do not understand a question or information.
- Read out loud to yourself—hearing what you are trying to learn is often helpful.
- Break large assignments into smaller pieces.
- Create a timeline for assignment completeness.
- Draw simple pictures to help solve story problems.
- Ask for uncluttered worksheets.
- Use a whiteboard as necessary.
- Use rhythm or music to help memorize facts.

- Solve similar problems at the same time; for example, solve all addition problems before solving subtraction problems.
- Seek support when needed.
- Remember to think about your future so you can maximize your education in the present.

REFERENCES

Cavenagh, S. (2008, November). Playing games in class helps students grasp math. *Education Digest, 74*(3), 43–46.

Cole, J. E., & Wasburn-Moses, L. H. (2010, March/April). Going beyond "The math wars": A special educator's guide to understanding and assisting with inquiry-based teaching in mathematics. *Teaching Exceptional Children, 42*(4), 14–20.

Crouse, S. L. (2010). *Dyscalculia (or dyscalcula): What it is and what it isn't.* Retrieved from http://www.ldinfo.com/dyscalculia.htm.

Doabler, C. T, Cary, M. S., Jungjohann, K., Clarke, B., Fien, H., Baker, S., Smolkowski, K., & Chard, D. (2012, March/April). Enhancing core mathematics instruction for students at risk for mathematics disabilities. *Teaching Exceptional Children, 44*(4), 48–57.

Miller, S. P., Stringfellow, J. L., Kaffar, B. J., Ferreira, D., & Mancl, D. B. (2011, November/December). Developing computation competence among students who struggle with mathematics. *Teaching Exceptional Children, 44*(2), 38–46.

Schwartz, A. E. (2007, October). New standards for improving two-year mathematics instruction. *Education Digest, 73*(2), 39–42.

Chapter 11

Final Thoughts and Flagship Moments

Writing this book has been a very enriching experience. The interviewees herein are indeed exceptional; they have been successful in spite of their "label." Being bullied, called "lazy" or "stupid," and being treated differently from their peers, these individuals have displayed extreme resiliency, confirming that achievement is within everyone's reach.

There were some dispiriting themes for exceptional students that appeared to be universal within this population. Many were bullied, called names, or excluded from participating with their peers in their daily classes or when on field trips. They felt isolated with few, if any, real friends. If a student had a visible disability such as an orthopedic or visual impairment, it was frequently and incorrectly assumed that he or she lacked intelligence. If a student had an invisible disability, it was assumed he or she was "stupid" or "lazy." Too often, insufficient staff collaboration resulted in inconsistent support as students navigated between classes and were promoted to the next grade. Many students describe their educational experience as one lacking teacher empathy.

"Resource class" frequently meant receiving work below the student's ability or receiving no work at all. Furthermore, being placed into general education classes but then having to physically walk out to attend resource class was perceived as very embarrassing. Often, the significance of a particular accommodation was not clearly described to the student; therefore, the full benefit was frequently not attained. Sometimes a school's administration, counseling department, or ancillary staff was unaware that a student had an individualized education program (IEP); if they did know, the strategies delineated were not consistently implemented. Alarmingly, very few students attended their IEP meetings or were involved in any decisions regarding their education or transition goals.

In due course, these experiences resulted in students' having to devise ways to fend for themselves. Sometimes their strategies were successful, such as that of the young man in the wheelchair who worked in the library when participating in physical education was considered to be awkward by his teacher, or the young man who worked in the cafeteria to avoid being bullied. Sometimes their strategies invited more negative attention, as in the case of the young man who laid his head on his desk with his arms over his head in order to not be involved in his unruly classmates' mischief.

On the other hand, some very appropriate tactics were implemented by teachers. These included giving students a quiet environment as needed that enabled them to focus, providing extra time to process and complete work, delivering instructions via multiple approaches that incorporated different learning styles (auditory, visual, and tactile), and describing tasks in concrete terms. Checking in with a designated person on a regular basis offered encouragement and provided a sense of belonging. Additionally, when students were encouraged to ask questions for clarification, they gained self-confidence. Having the opportunity to participate in age-appropriate activities with peers who had similar conditions, for example, wheelchairs, was viewed as beneficial. Also, many students reported that hands-on activities helped them understand concepts. Enthusiastic teachers generated an enthusiastic environment.

Successful outcomes are evidenced as the interviewees transitioned from high school to the workplace or college. The result of each individual's tenacity was that many goals were realized. Some students have chosen to work in a professional business environment. Others are becoming educators themselves, believing that their experiences will enrich the lives they touch. Still others are working in trades such as construction or vehicle repair, receiving valuable on-the-job training. No matter what route is chosen, their journeys are both challenging and rewarding.

For parents, dispiriting themes stemmed from teachers not intervening as soon as a problem was noted (whether it was behavioral or academic), and teachers failing to praise the child when a task with which the child struggled immensely was accomplished. Parents often felt unheard when they discussed their concerns or frustrations and believe they were frequently talked to in a patronizing manner. Having to repeatedly advocate for their child, often within the same setting and with the same staff members, was very overwhelming and exhausting.

The absence of teachers and ancillary staff at IEP meetings implied a lack of caring. When those who were in attendance failed to ensure that parents understood the terms spoken, parents felt patronized. Several parents recalled multiple teachers who acted aloof to the struggles and needs of their child. These parents resented the implication that their children were condemned to live a substandard life and that they, as parents, simply needed to come to terms with that fact and lower the expectations of what their children might accomplish in the future. Realizing months after the meeting's conclusion that the strategies discussed were not being implemented, the parents felt demoralized about the education system as a whole.

Parents were upset that the government required their child to be labeled as a "student with a disability" in order to receive services, as this seemed to imply there was an inability to learn or function in the same setting as the child's peers, which in turn greatly affected their child's self-esteem. Although the intent of the law is to provide supportive services, having a label indicated to both parent and child that the child was different. It was also discouraging that schools seemed to have a one-program-fits-all approach when it came to "fixing" a problem; for example, all students were on an academic track without the option of learning a trade or skill. Many parents were surprised to learn that their child should have received information about various organizations that could help their child transition from high school to the postsecondary world.

On the other hand, parents believe that having a trusted person for their child to check in with on a regular basis and having extra time to process information and complete tasks was helpful. All believe that the earlier the correct intervention is started, the better the outcome will be. They also believe that praise is one of the greatest motivators. When received, it can light a spark that would otherwise not exist. Most parents believe their lives are richer because of the inspiration received from watching their child succeed in a turbulent system.

In this book, a humble group of exceptional people have bared their souls. These individuals fervently hope they have imparted information that will aid in your endeavor to seek and implement meaningful strategies for yourself and for those with whom you interact. Empowerment is understanding that you, a single person with resolve, can make a significant difference for yourself and those around you. Within a society, giving more than one takes is a requiem to the human spirit. Below is a summary of these flagship moments.

TEACHERS

- Do not rely on your current knowledge—be willing to expand it and learn different techniques to help your students.
- Help students build friendships. They are just like everyone else and want to be part of a group with similar interests and desires.
- Capitalize on student strengths so learning is fun.

- Apprise yourself of a student's situation so you are helping avoid embarrassment, for example, by insisting on timed tests for someone with a processing issue.
- Teach organizational skills; exceptional students often require much effort to get organized.
- Be approachable; caring makes a difference.
- Provide a predictable, consistent, fair environment.
- Reward effort, not just results; note steady improvement.
- Instill fearlessness; exceptional students know they are "different" and need you to guide them when they feel alone or overwhelmed.
- Inspire students to learn new information as appropriate; they may act as though they do not want to work hard, but we all remember the stimulating teacher who made a difference in our lives.
- Avoid inflating grades; this practice helps no one.
- Ensure that students have a designated place to go if they are upset or just need to talk to someone.
- Be enthusiastic and passionate—it's contagious.
- Remember that exceptional students often see and process the world differently; be open to their perspective and collaboratively create supports that lead to successful outcomes.
- Avoid sounding arrogant when communicating with parents and students; let your professional compassion and knowledge guide you during collaborative efforts.
- Impart information on organizations that can provide support at various junctures.
- Familiarize yourself with a student's medication and its effect, for example, lethargy, loss of appetite, or inability to focus, to name a few.
- Listen to parents without judging their choices—this journey is new to them and they are doing their best to navigate an unfamiliar system with limited knowledge.
- Discuss issues regarding a student's exceptionality in private, not within another student's hearing.
- Permit and encourage the use of accommodations and modifications that are in a student's IEP; they have been agreed to by a team of professionals and agreed to by the parent(s) and student.
- Practice inclusion to the greatest extent possible within the continuum of services; everyone benefits from this strategy when it is implemented correctly.
- Discuss postsecondary goals and ensure that coursework prepares the student for them.
- Earning one's way into a higher-level class is thrilling; however, the change in placement should occur during a natural break to avoid embarrassment.

- Praise frequently.

PARENTS

- If you suspect a problem exists, get your child evaluated as soon as possible; the earlier an intervention begins, the greater the success.
- Advocate tirelessly for your child.
- Proactively keep yourself in the loop by contacting teachers and asking about your child's progress.
- Help your child learn how to socialize.
- Remember that children often convey their thoughts and feelings through their moods, attitudes, and body language—not necessarily through their words.
- Discuss issues involving romance; impairment does not negate natural desires.
- Learn about your parental rights.
- Ensure that IEPs are appropriate and are being implemented; if unsure, take a trusted third party like a friend or relative to the meeting to ask questions.
- If you don't know what tests were administered, why, and their results, ask the school psychologist to clarify. If you desire additional testing, request it (written requests are the best approach).
- Get to know your child's support staff (aides)—they can be instrumental in providing what your child requires.
- If you don't know something, ask. If the explanation is unclear, get clarification.
- Support your child's endeavors.
- Provide choices and let your child learn from natural consequences.
- Be aware that prescription medications usually need to be closely monitored and that doses or the prescription itself may need to change frequently.
- If your child is on medication, ensure that it is taken as prescribed.
- Seek professional guidance but remember that you know your child better than anyone.
- Be honest about your child's needs—refusing to do so impedes progress.
- Establish a routine—this is reassuring to a child as it provides predictable parameters within which to function.
- Ensure that your child has some fun time.
- Seek opportunities that will provide various experiences.

- Brainstorm creative alternatives to meet your child's needs, for example, adaptive PE for physical education course credit, becoming a teacher's aide or library assistant.
- Ask for assistive technology if it would benefit your child.
- Gather information about Individuals with Disabilities Education Act (IDEA) versus the Americans with Disabilities Act (ADA) in the college environment; support services are vastly different in college and high school.
- Ask about organizations that can help your child transition from high school to the work world, trade school, or college environment.

STUDENTS

- Embrace who you are and focus on your strengths; remember that we all learn differently.
- Believe in yourself and dismiss the naysayers; don't give your power away to them.
- Participate in groups that revolve around your interests.
- Share your exceptionality or impairment with others—it will help them understand what is unique about you (thankfully, we are all unique in various ways).
- After an experience, reflect on the positive aspects of what can be learned.
- Take advantage of accommodations in your IEP—they are there to help you.
- Practice time management and get organized by creating a calendar of tasks and sticking to it.
- Dream big and use every resource at your disposal.
- Ask a question when you don't understand what was said; you often help others as well as yourself.
- Observe successful people and imitate what they do to be effective.
- Organize your time by using a calendar to record when assignments are due.
- Complete your homework even if it seems useless; it reinforces what was taught and helps the information transfer into your long-term memory for later recall.
- Get to know your teachers—the more face time you have with them, the more they learn about you and how to support your needs.
- Attend your IEP meetings—they are about you: your needs, goals, and strategies to help you be successful.

- Discuss your postsecondary desires with your teachers and counselors and learn about organizations that can assist you with your transition from high school.
- Work hard—success occurs when preparedness meets opportunity.
- You may feel as if you have to work two to three times harder than your classmates to learn the same information or to complete a task. Often, however, there is someone without an exceptionality who has to work just as hard as you, so stay focused and positive.
- Do what you love and have a passion for; money does not buy happiness.
- Reflect on activities you like to do as a hobby—this can be indicative of your future career path.
- Find an enjoyable activity that helps you decompress and vent at the same time, such as a physical education, music, or art class.
- Time flies—it is not a renewable resource and cannot be recovered when gone, so use it wisely.
- Find the good in everyone and avoid gossip; when people are born, they do not have the power to decide what their skin or eye color is, how tall they will be, the size of their nose, or their intellectual abilities—teasing others about such matters is a waste of energy.
- Invite the outsider to join your group of friends; such kindness has immeasurable internal rewards.
- Accomplishing goals may require adjusting strategies, for example, one may lose some vision, hearing, or physical abilities. Be flexible and patient—you can achieve your goals.

About the Author

Dr. Faith Andreasen has over twenty years of educational experience, teaching elementary- through college-level students. She served as a department chair for special education and has mentored graduate students in leadership and special education courses. Dr. Andreasen is a former associate professor of research at Northcentral University and has been published in several peer-reviewed journals. In addition, she is an alternative dispute resolution mediator.